Prais

"Pastor Jacob Rodriguez does it again; this is a brilliant piece of work! This story is gripping, the narrative is eloquent, and the theology is sound. You will not be able to put this book down! Yielding to temptations is an everyday issue that we all face, and a very delicate one at that. I believe this book will be an instrument for discussion within the body of Christ and educators alike. I highly recommend *Lying Lions* to anyone who desires to understand and break free from their temptations."

—DR. JOHN FORTINO, Presiding Bishop,
Apostolic Assembly of the Faith in Christ Jesus

"*Lying Lions* is a masterpiece writing that every Christian who desires to crucify this flesh must read. It deals with the silent lions in our lives that keep us from living our Christian life to its maximum potential. It provides the biblical tools to overcome our silent lions and live a triumphant life."

—BISHOP JOE PRADO, senior pastor & bishop,
Apostolic Assembly, East Palo Alto, CA

"In our society today, young and old face many challenges and temptations. *Lying Lions* will serve as a great encouragement and guide on how to navigate through the obstacles and challenges life presents. I truly am convinced that you cannot complete this book without being empowered, encouraged and changed!"

—DR. MARK AMIN, youth pastor,
Bakersfield Apostolic Church, Bakersfield, CA

"*Lying Lions* is a must-read for all young, traveling preachers. It's a fresh view of a timely piece of scripture. It's relevant in today's culture. This helps unmask the snares of the enemy and equips the readers with tools to overcome."
—OMAR CORTEZ, senior pastor,
Christian Tabernacle, Houston, TX

"*Lying Lions* is a narrative masterpiece on the dangers of secret temptations. From beginning to end, Pastor Jacob masterfully and skillfully ministers to the very soul of every believer's daily battle with the inevitable reality of temptation. Regardless of your level of spiritual maturity, Lying Lions has a word for you! It's a must read book for all ages. Congratulations Pastor Jacob, for another inspirational and timely message to the world of Christianity."
—BISHOP JOSEPH V. RODRIGUEZ, senior pastor & bishop,
Community Christian Church, San Jose, CA

"In a very encouraging way, Pastor Jacob Rodriguez helps the reader confront their area of temptation and also provides practical steps to overcoming it. Although for many this is a taboo topic, the author sheds light not only on the need to discuss it, but on the possibility of living free. If you desire to live a victorious life, then the Lying Lions is the right book for you."
—ANTHONY ROMO, assistant pastor,
Phoenix First Apostolic Church, Phoenix, AZ

"*Lying Lions* by Jacob Rodriguez is truly a gift of deliverance. He uncovers game-changing insight into the temptation we all face and delivers powerful, Biblical strategies for being more than a conqueror. The truth you acknowledge will make you free. Jacob helps us to do just that—acknowledge the truth of God's Word regarding temptation and it's application to our lives today!"
—AARON BARBOSA, recording artist & worship leader,
Apostolic Worship Epicenter, Baldwin Park, CA

"In this day and age if we do not have proper Godly Spiritual guidance in our lives, then there is no proper solution to the carnal deceptive side of man. Jacob Rodriguez has brought to us that solution and has unveiled the lustful nature of man by bringing a clarion call to all who will listen and be guided into understanding that true pleasures lie in a living God who challenges us to conquer ourselves and not live satisfied with the fatal, temporal pleasures that lie in a carcass experience. "
—MIKE ORTEGA, senior pastor,
New Beginnings Church, Columbus, OH

JACOB M. RODRIGUEZ

LYING LIONS

Finding Freedom
in a World of Temptation

Lying Lions
© 2014 by Jacob M. Rodriguez

Published by CityLight Church Publications
Edited by David Avila
Cover design by TMG Design Studio

ISBN-13: 978-1502371317
ISBN-10: 1502371316

All Scripture quotations, unless otherwise specified, are from the New International Version of the Bible. Copyright © 1973, 1978, 1984, International Bible Society.

Scripture quotations marked NKJV are from the New King James Version of the Bible. Copyright © 1979, 1980, 1982 by Thomas Nelson, Inc., publishers.

All rights reserved. No part of this publication may be reproduced, stored in a retrieval system, or transmitted in any form or by any means—electronic, mechanical, photocopying, recording, scanning or otherwise—except for brief quotations in reviews or articles, without written permission.

Emphasis within Scripture is the author's own. Please note that the author's writing style is to capitalize certain pronouns in Scripture and text that refer to God, and may differ from other religious publishers' styles. The author chose to acknowledge Him, even to the point of violating grammatical rules.

Dedication

This book is dedicated to the church I have the joy and honor of pastoring—

CityLight Church, Mountain View, CA

Books by Jacob Rodriguez

The Woman's Touch

The Lord's Lady

Hidden Kings

Someone Like Me

Crave

Shift

Contents

1. A Lion's Tale / 11
The Dangers of Secret Temptations

2. Then *Stings* My Soul / 21
Understanding Why we Sin

3. Temptation Triggers / 31
Understanding Why we're Tempted

4. Canceled Fights / 47
The Consequences of Giving Up

5. Purge the Urge / 63
Strategies for Personal Purity

6. Who Do You Think You Are? / 81
Unlocking your True Identity

7. Untamed Emotions / 99
Controlling your Feelings and Impulses

8. When you Pray / 117
Deepening your Conversations with Jesus

9. Breaking your Silence / 131
Finding Freedom through Confession

10. Lion Killers / 151
Facing your Fears with Courage

11. The Roaring Lamb / 165
Following Jesus into Victory

Acknowledgements / 179
About the Author / 181

1
A Lion's Tale

The Dangers of Secret Temptations

Pat yourself on the back. The fact that you saw the title of this book and still opened it up deserves a little pat on the back—seriously. You're probably thinking: *Why? I haven't even read the book yet.* Well, you're right. But with a title like *Lying Lions*, I figured it took some guts to even buy or open the book.

From a book-selling standpoint, I probably didn't do myself any favors by a) writing a book about temptation – a subject that people avoid, and b) choosing an unflinching title. However, you deserve to know what you're getting yourself into. There's no backdoor approach to this subject without it becoming vague and meaningless. Some issues just have to be tackled head-on despite our fears and assumptions about it. But I can assure you, this book is not just about temptation; it's about God's calling and purpose for your life.

In this era of feel-good Theology and self-importance, nobody wants to hear about their sins. In fact, we mistakenly re-label sins and call them *mistakes*.

Concepts like *sin* and *temptation* are becoming too messy for the modern believer. People don't want to hear about how bad and dysfunctional they are; we only want to hear about how good and generous we are. This isn't a rant, but a diagnosis of our human nature and how quickly truth is fading in our culture.

Temptation is not a trendy subject, it's a touchy subject. For some, it causes flashbacks to a hurtful situation or irreversible decision. For some, it strikes fear about a secret struggle at work, at the gym, at home or even at church. For some, temptation exposes un-surrendered areas that plague spiritual growth. For some, it touches a nerve of shame and guilt, because it feels dirty just being tempted (even if there was no sin).

For all of us, temptation is real and unavoidable. But it doesn't have to defeat you! God has your back, and He's given you powerful weapons to overcome temptation and live in victory.

That Lyon is Lyin'

Despite this book's title, it's not about African Safaris or wildlife. I chose this title based on a scene in the life of Samson, which I believe illustrates the secret dangers of temptation. In case you're wondering, it's not the story about Delilah. As provocative as it is, Samson's downfall with Delilah along with the infamous buzz cut was triggered by decisions earlier in his life. Samson's female problems were simply the tip of the iceberg, the late stages of a problem he never dealt with.

The scene is found in Judges 14:5-9. Please read it below:

"Samson went down to Timnah together with his father and mother. As they approached the vineyards of Timnah, suddenly a young lion came roaring toward him. The Spirit of the LORD came powerfully upon him so that he tore the lion

apart with his bare hands as he might have torn a young goat. But he told neither his father nor his mother what he had done. Then he went down and talked with the woman, and he liked her. Some time later, when he went back to marry her, he turned aside to look at the lion's carcass, and in it he saw a swarm of bees and some honey. He scooped out the honey with his hands and ate as he went along. When he rejoined his parents, he gave them some, and they too ate it. But he did not tell them that he had taken the honey from the lion's carcass."

The story of Samson is very popular. He was a man with unlimited potential. He was set aside by God for a holy purpose and was given a supernatural gift of strength. Samson was truly a beast in a man's body.

In the story above, Samson's supernatural strength was displayed when he killed a roaring lion with his bare hands. Can you imagine that scene? I would have loved ringside seats to that fight...*if you can even call it a fight.* Technically, this was a slaughter, not a fight. No Kung-Fu tricks necessary. Samson tore the lion apart like a newborn goat. The lion had no idea what *beast* it was up against.

This event was also the first time Samson used his gift of strength. He was barely discovering his God-given abilities. This was his debut – a glimpse of his destiny.

I imagine after he slayed the lion, he gazed at his bloody hands and realized what had just happened. His inner stirring had finally manifested. That's a great feeling, when what's stirring inside of you – your potential, your gift – is unleashed.

But the story didn't end there.

The same lion that Samson killed at one point in his journey was used to entrap him at another point. He may have displayed his dominance over the *roaring* lion, but his real struggle was with the *silent* lion.

The second fight with the lion wasn't technically a fight either. In fact, Samson didn't even put up a fight. He saw something sweet inside the lion's carcass and took it without hesitation. As a Nazarite, Samson had made a vow never to touch dead flesh. Scooping out honey from a dead lion was a clear violation of his covenant with God. In other words, this wasn't a grey area for Samson. He knowingly disobeyed God's command. The temptation of the silent lion's honey was so enticing, so sweet, he just couldn't resist.

It was the *lying* lion that got him to compromise. Lying down dead and lying with deception. That lion was lyin' to him alright!

Secret Lions

It's the silent struggles and temptations that pose the greatest threat to our lives. Secret, silent lions like pride and lust can slip into our hearts and destroy us from the inside out. Samson knew this reality all too well.

The Bible mentions that Samson had two separate opportunities to tell his parents about this lion. The first time, "...he told neither his father nor his mother what he had done" (v.6). The second time, "...he did not tell them that he had taken the honey from the lion's carcass" (v.9).

I can understand Samson's rationale for not telling his family about his second encounter with the lion. He was hiding a dirty secret.

But why wouldn't he mention or celebrate his first encounter with the lion? When you get a raise or promotion at work, usually you can't wait to share the good news with your loved ones. When my son Makai brings home a good report card from school, we celebrate his accomplishments. When he's playing baseball (T-ball), we cheer like crazy for every little thing he does. Accomplishments, big or small, should be celebrated.

Samson fought and killed a lion with his bare hands, but was totally mum about it.

Why would anyone hide such a great victory? We can only guess why he didn't celebrate it. But since wine was also off limits to Nazarites, and he was strolling through a vineyard, maybe he was afraid that celebrating would be an admission of guilt. It would be like a Christian helping put out a fire at a night club. Celebrating your good deed would open up questions about why you were there in the first place.

Whatever his reasons were, his silence about the first fight made it easier to be silent about the second fight.

Uncelebrated victories inspire the enemy. What you're not willing to celebrate becomes a reentry point for the enemy to strike again. Because, what you don't celebrate openly, you're not accountable to defend privately. Celebrating the defeat of the lion in round one could have curbed Samson's curiosity in round two. Since no one knew about his private victory, no one would question him about his private failure.

Many of us react strongly to ferocious problems (roaring lions), but struggle with silent temptations (lying lions).

When lions roar against us, we fight back – we pray harder, worship louder and band together. Roaring lions make their presence known. They want to strike fear into people. No question, that's the devil's job description.

1 Peter 5:8 tells us, *"Be sober, be vigilant; because your adversary the devil walks about like a roaring lion, seeking whom he may devour."* We forget how cunning the devil can be. Sometimes he chases, and sometimes he lies and waits.

God warned Cain, *"...if you do not do what is right, sin is crouching at your door; it desires to have you, but you must rule over it"* (Genesis 4:7). This picture of temptation is like a crouching lion, waiting silently and patiently. This lion isn't running or roaring loudly at you—it's lying down waiting for you to step into its turf.

After Cain's offering was disregarded, he had an opportunity to learn from his mistake. Instead, his emotions boiled. When God confronted Cain, he was vulnerable and about to change the course of history in the most negative way. Regrettably, Cain didn't listen to God's warning and soon enough, had his brother's blood on his hands.

Satan doesn't always roar, but he's always hunting.

- Are you aware of any secret lions in your life?
- Are you faced with a secret temptation at work, at school, or even at home?
- Are you carrying secret shame and condemnation?
- Are you battling secret feelings of depression, regret, or bitterness?
- Has a family secret been eating away at your peace of mind?
- Is there a silent lion of doubt or fear controlling your life?
- Are you hiding any secret addictions or habits from your spouse or family?
- Have you ever tried to tell someone about your secret struggle but chickened out at the last minute?

Sorry for not warning you about all those questions. I understand if you're ready to close this book and toss it under your bed. Things are already getting very personal, and it's only the first chapter. But don't worry. I can't read your mind or predict your situation. This book won't work unless you get honest about yourself and the real issues (lions) you're facing.

You shouldn't be ashamed to admit personal temptation. As I'll explain in the coming chapters, *everyone* gets tempted. Keep reading and you'll discover the root of temptation – why it comes, when it comes, and how it comes. It's time to gain the edge over the enemy and defeat those lying lions!

2

Then *Stings* My Soul

Understanding Why we Sin

You may have never heard of Michael Smith (no, not Christian songwriter and singer). This Michael Smith is a scientist who wanted to know the answer to a question that most bee researchers' ponder, but wouldn't dare to experiment – "Where is the most painful place to be stung?" My initial thought is, *some questions are better left unanswered.*

But Smith, who devotes his studies to the behavior of honeybees, decided this mystery needed to be solved once and for all.

So, in the name of science, he stung himself 190 times in various body parts to find the answer.

For 38 days, Smith would pick up a bee by its wings and hold that little honey-making buzzer on the place he was testing for pain. Then, he would keep the stinger in place for a full minute. Smith rated the pain on a scale of 1 to 10. Before ending his research, Smith had stung himself in 25 different body parts—three times each.

Ouch! Maybe your job isn't that bad after all.

The shuttering results of his study revealed the most painful place to be stung was, unexpectedly, the nose. The pain of getting stung on the nose was ranked 9 out of 10. Hats off to Mr. Smith. I don't know anyone who would volunteer himself for that kind of pain – science or not.

Smith's research reminds me of one of my earliest and most painful childhood memories. I must have been around six or seven years old.

It was during a summer camping trip with my family. One night just before bed I was inside my tent when all of the sudden I felt a sharp needle-like pain jabbing into my forearm. After a couple of seconds, the pain became like a hot knife searing my skin. You guessed it—a bee stung me.

And oh yeah, I was screaming my head off in horror.

Then I heard the footsteps of my dad running towards the tent. He immediately pulled me out and whisked me away into the arms of my grandma who was sitting nearby. She tried rubbing mud on the sting (an old home remedy), but it barely helped. Moments later my dad discovered the little yellow culprit hiding inside the tent.

It was the first and only time I've ever been stung; and I'd like to keep it that way. Bee stings are very painful, which begs the question: *why would Samson voluntarily stick his hand into a beehive...just for a little glob of honey?*

Between Hornets and Help

What captivated Samson wasn't a dead lion, but the honey inside the carcass. As he passed by the lion, he noticed a swarm of bees buzzing around it. The honey was the lure, and the carcass was the sin. But let's back up a little in Samson's life, even before his rumble with the lion. It seems like flying stingers were swarming in his life from an early age.

Judges 13:24-25 says, "The woman gave birth to a boy and named him Samson. He grew and the LORD blessed him, and the Spirit of the LORD began to stir him while he was in Mahaneh Dan, between Zorah and Eshtaol."

According to the text, God's Spirit began to stir Samson while he was living between Zorah and Eshtaol. The Hebrew name Zorah means "hornet or bee." And the name Eshtaol means "asking for help."

It's interesting that Samson stood between a "hornet" and "asking God for help." Like him, we all face situations where we stand between two choices. As we walk through life, we are confronted with decisions that will either advance or delay our purpose. In a sense, we can either get stung by a bee (hornet) or ask God for help.

Between getting stung and getting help, God's Spirit was stirring and moving Samson. I'd like to propose that God is doing the same for you. As you stand between decisions, confronted with healthy and harmful choices, the Holy Spirit wants to stir His purpose in your life. God wants to lead you in the direction of His perfect will. As you stand between hornets and help, between right and wrong, the Holy Spirit is working.

Samson was hypnotized by the honey, which made him ignore the pain of being stung. I wonder if you have ever been hypnotized by greed or envy? I wonder if you have ever lost sight of what matters most, to pursue what matters little. When we're tempted, we could easily reach a point when we ignore the pain that our choices will cause us and those we care about.

I can picture Samson standing over the lion's carcass and the swarm of bees circling and landing on his hand. Now, I realize that I'm using a creative license. We don't actually know if the bees stung him. But whether they did or not isn't the point. The real issue is that he willingly placed himself in harms way—that he didn't care. His eyes informed his brain that touching the beehive was dangerous—but it didn't matter. Once his craving took over, his logic was paralyzed. Even if the honeybees didn't sting him, he was still stung by sin.

Hunger Games

As Samson licked the honey off his sticky fingers, he hadn't just lost a physical test, but a spiritual test. He came into contact with the ultimate stinger of sin. The bible reveals in 1 Corinthians 15:56, *"The sting of death is sin, and the power of sin is the law."* Sin stings because with it comes the unpleasant reality of consequence and judgment. A bee stings your skin, but sin stings your soul.

I don't think sin needs to be redefined, but re-understood. Throughout this book I will tackle various issues about sin, including how to confess your sins and be forgiven. But oftentimes "sin" becomes a catch-all term that doesn't bring enough clarity for personal change. We know God hates sin. We know unsaved sinners won't inherit the kingdom of God. We know sin destroys lives.

We know what sin *does* – it's consequences. But do we know what sin *is*? Our prepackaged Sunday School answer is usually that *sin is disobeying God's commands*. That is the safest and truest definition. But it doesn't quite address the reasons why we sin. Theologically speaking, we are all born sinners, since we are descendants of Adam—the original sinner. Because of our sinful nature, we all have a proclivity towards sin.

Three-year-old children will lie to their parents, not because someone taught them how to lie, but because sin and iniquity are in our genes. David revealed, *"Surely I was sinful at birth, sinful from the time my mother conceived me"* (Psalm 51:5). By nature, we sin because we are fallen people living in a fallen world. The theology of sin deals with our state of sinfulness and need for a Savior—since we are utterly incapable of washing our own sins away. However, I would like you to also consider the psychology of sin – the internal forces that lead us to sinful choices.

Sin is meeting legitimate needs in illegitimate ways. In other words, our attempts to satisfy our inner cravings without God lead to sin. In Samson's case, he was hungry. He didn't wake up that morning and say, "Today is a good day to sin and compromise my vows. What kind of trouble do I want to get myself into?" He didn't plan on sinning – but he did plan on eating (just like we all do). Hunger represents emptiness, a void that yearns to be filled. This is when temptation strikes.

Satan used honey to appeal to Samson's hunger. He leveraged a legitimate human need with an illegitimate way of fulfilling it. Every area of life that hungers must be redeemed and filled by the Spirit of God. Our souls must feed from the bread of God's Word. But Satan's job is to pervert our hunger and use it against us. He even used this tactic against Jesus, *"If you are the Son of God, tell these stones to become bread"* (Matthew 4:3). I'll develop this thought more in the next chapter. This hunger game of temptation is one of life and death, defeat and victory.

Fallen Arrows

The prevalent Greek word for "sin" in the New Testament epistles is *hamartia,* which referred to the bulls-eye of a target. Essentially, sin is *missing the mark,* because no one hits the bulls-eye every time. Paul used this Greek term when he wrote, *"for all have sinned and fall short of the glory of God"* (Romans 3:23). In other words, everyone has *missed the mark* as an archer's arrow strikes the ground because it fell short of its target.

However, the arrow still hits somewhere with the same velocity and impact. Like a stinger, the arrow's point still punctures and does damage. There is a price for missing the mark—one that pierces the soul. If the arrow doesn't hit its target, something or someone else has to absorb the impact. Missing the mark is part of being human. But it shouldn't be an excuse to live recklessly or to avoid responsibility for those you've hurt.

If you're missing the mark, it's time to get real and recognize your shortcomings. Pick up the fallen arrows. Recover what's been lost—in you or your family. If you're a parent, especially, you have an obligation to deal with your fallen arrows (and stingers) and overcome temptation for the next generation.

The bible says, *"Like arrows in the hands of a warrior are children born in one's youth"* (Psalm 127:4). Sin affects where we aim our children, where they end up. If I continue to miss the mark because I'm negligent or selfish, my kids will struggle to hit the mark themselves. We can't be perfect, but we shouldn't settle for average. If we don't deal with our vices, we will hand them down to our sons and daughters.

You won't always hit the target—but at least aim in the right direction.

The purpose of this short chapter was to help you think more clearly about sin and its sting. Like Samson, we're often standing at the intersection of difficult choices. As you turn the pages, you're going to discover why we are tempted. You'll also see Christ more clearly, the One who defeated the sting of sin and death.

LYING LIONS

3

Temptation Triggers

Understanding Why we're Tempted

Samson found himself in a sticky situation, literally. On his way back to Timnah "he turned aside to look at the lion's carcass, and in it he saw a swarm of bees and some honey. He scooped out the honey with his hands and ate as he went along..." (Judges 14:8-9). On the surface, this is a classic example of temptation. He saw something he wasn't supposed to see, he touched something he was forbidden to touch, and he took something he didn't need.

Case closed.

It's that simple.

And it's also that complicated.

Temptation is as old as the earth itself. It's tightly threaded into the story of humanity, from the Garden of Eden until now. It's a daily reality that we all face. In fact, no human is exempt or given a free pass. As long as you're alive, you will be tempted. As long as sin and evil are present in the world, temptation will have a job.

I used to think that the closer you were to God, the less tempted you were – as if God has some cosmic sin-repellant that He sprays on the faithful. Maybe you assume that the more spiritual you become, the fewer temptations and trials you'll have. The truth is, we are never fully immune from the reality of temptation.

Jesus said, *"Pray that you will not fall into temptation"* (Luke 22:40). In His model prayer, He said, *"lead us not into temptation, but deliver us from the evil one"* (Matthew 6:13). There's a difference between being tempted and falling into temptation.

Let me remind you of something we know, but seem to forget. *Jesus was tempted.*

Want to read it again? Go for it.

Now, I know we know this. But we tend to fast forward to Jesus' winning strategies without fully absorbing the reality that He was tempted. Hebrews 4:15 states that Jesus was, "...*tempted in every way, just as we are—yet was without sin.*" It's true that He didn't sin, but realize that Jesus faced off with the most common human experience.

I'm drilling this point because too often, we discredit ourselves for experiencing something that is humanly normal. We have developed misbeliefs based on the lies that Satan interjects into our minds. For many believers, being tempted *feels like a sin*. So, they carry around false guilt and self-condemnation. True guilt can be positive if it leads to repentance. But false guilt about false sins is a lose-lose situation. Temptation is not a sin. It's a lure to sin.

Being tempted doesn't make you strange or a second-class Christian, it makes you human.

I'm going to write something that might sound like a contradiction to what I just wrote. Everyone is tempted, but not *equally* tempted.

Temptations are everywhere. But becoming a born-again believer transfers you into God's kingdom and empowers you with the mission of saving others. Therefore, you pose a threat to the kingdom of darkness. Your adversary takes notice and you become a target.

Unmasking the Tempter

Random temptations are a myth. There's no such thing. The truth is, behind every temptation is a tempter who is engineering a well-timed, well-planned attack. They are below-the-belt punches intended to destroy your life. In Samson's case, the lion's honey may seem like a coincidence. But when you are chosen by God and filled with His awesome power, there are no accidental attacks.

Honestly, I hate talking or writing about anything that embellishes our adversary. I think in some cases we exaggerate Satan's power for good theatrics, at the expense of good theology. Hollywood perpetuates this, too. It seems like the villains in every recent superhero movie is getting darker, more evil, and more powerful. And since Satan is viewed as humanity's ultimate villain, he benefits from all the propaganda. People consume those powerful images of evil and unknowingly ascribe the devil with the same kind of powers and abilities.

Satan is not a comic book super-villain with infinite powers. He's a defeated foe, a created being that fell from heaven like lightening and answers directly to God. Satan is not God's evil counterpart or equal. He's a doomed creature with fixed limitations. He can't read your mind. He can't be everywhere at the same time. Essentially, he's only as powerful as you allow him to be.

However, don't unlock your doors and disarm your alarm system just yet. Although Satan is a limited creature, he still roams the earth seeking to devour people. Satan is defeated, but not stupid. The opening pages of the Bible introduce a hyper-intelligent, highly calculated serpent (Genesis 3:1), a creature later described as a dragon (Revelation 12). Also, Satan doesn't work alone. He's got demonic forces and cronies that do a lot of his dirty work (Ephesians 6:10-12).

Satan's primary weapon is his mouth – which he uses skillfully to suggest, confuse, entice, accuse, condemn and lie. He doesn't just occasionally make false statements; he's utterly incapable of being truthful. Lying is his native language. It's all he knows how to do. Like a spider, he spools one web of lies after another. He is the father of lies (John 8:44).

It's no coincidence that when the devil came to tempt Jesus, he did so through dialogue – he opened his mouth and tried to deceive. It's the same thing he did to Adam and Eve. As I'll discuss later, the devil only has a few tricks in the bag, so not only does he devise a cunning strategy, he studies our behavior, our weaknesses and our propensities. He may not be ever-present like God, but he has enough intelligence about you to know when and where to strike.

What Triggers Temptation?

No one understands the devil's strategy better than Jesus. In the moments following His baptism, He drew some unwanted attention. Luke 4:1-2 says, *"Jesus, full of the Holy Spirit, returned from the Jordan and was led by the Spirit in the desert, where for forty days he was tempted by the devil He ate nothing during those days, and at the end of them he was hungry."* This clip from Jesus' life reveals three conditions that trigger temptations. Like Samson's honey, these conditions can lead to some sticky situations.

1. Spiritual Highs

Similar to Samson who was stirred by the Spirit (Judges 13:25), Jesus was on what we might call a "spiritual high." Just before being tempted, Jesus was baptized, saw the heavens open up, felt the Holy Spirit rest like a dove, and heard a voice from heaven saying, *"You are my Son, whom I love; with you I am well pleased"* (Luke 3:22). If that's not a spiritual high, I don't know what is.

Any one of those experiences would have been significant on its own. But having all four experiences (baptism, open heavens, a descended dove, and a voice of love and approval) occur in succession is overwhelming.

Imagine how loved and affirmed Jesus must have felt? Had that been me, I would have been walking on cloud nine and feeling like I was invincible. As a teenager, that's how I used to feel after the last night of youth camp – pumped, empowered, and ready to work. You feel like you're ready to take on the world.

Well, Jesus was ready to do exactly that – take on the world. And that caused some chatter. Not just on earth, but in hell. Some have this notion that when you repent, heaven applauds and hell boos. While it's true that heaven rejoices when one sinner repents (Luke 15:10), hell doesn't just protest by throwing rotten tomatoes – it throws flaming arrows (Eph. 6:16).

Temptation is a reaction to your relationship with God and your purpose. If you are playing a role in the kingdom, expect to be tempted. As the Holy Spirit moves in and through your life, hell's radar lights up and detects the power you carry. But the real danger comes when we ride the wave of good feelings and get too comfortable. Perhaps you feel so on-top-of-the-world that you think you're untouchable, that you say to yourself, "Surely, I can't be tempted now. I'm above that".

Pride rises.

Guards drop.

Temptation attacks.

This news shouldn't frighten you, but embolden you to take your relationship with God serious and gain the edge on temptation.

The intensity of temptation rises in proportion to your level of influence in the kingdom. Ask Joseph, the young dreamer who fled the seduction of Potiphar's wife. Ask Gehazi, the prophet's assistant who couldn't tame his greed.

Ask David, an accomplished king who got lazy and couldn't resist a bathing woman named Bathsheba. Ask Nehemiah, who resisted the temptation to quit on his dreams. In each case, whether a good or bad example, temptation grew in parallel with their spiritual success.

Jesus was no exception in this regard. Before His clothes could dry from the Jordan River, temptation schemes were already being drawn up in the devil's playbook. But Jesus was ready. He wouldn't be duped or caught off guard. Now, maybe you're thinking, "Wait a minute, I'm not Jesus! I don't know if I can be that strong in the moment." Don't worry. As you'll continue to discover in the pages of this book, God is with you. He's giving you plenty of ammo to fight back.

The key is to know the enemy's moves and how to overcome those sticky situations.

2. Loneliness

Like Samson who wandered alone towards the lion, Jesus found Himself alone in the wilderness. In fact, He was alone for a total of forty days. Satan saw this as an opportunity to strike.

God has allowed me to travel and minister quite extensively in the last six years or so. I've crisscrossed this nation many times and have enjoyed the blessing of meeting different people and ministering in all types of settings – large and small. I love visiting places. But honestly, traveling alone got old real fast. I tip my hat to those traveling preachers and businessmen who can spend days, if not weeks, on the road. It's not easy.

Call me what you want, but after just a couple of days of being away from my family and home, I'm barely hanging on. I've never gotten used to empty hotel rooms and crowded airports. But when my wife Cherie and the kids join me, it's a different story. I'm a much happier guy.

It's being alone that doesn't appeal to me. And I've also noticed that being alone or isolated makes me more vulnerable to spiritual attack. Since no one is around to see what I'm doing, the temptation to sin is more convenient. The voice that says, "No one will ever find out" gets louder.

Of course, we can't always avoid being alone. Sometimes, God leads us into lonely seasons in order to test our faith or narrow the aperture of our focus on Him. Being alone helps us de-clutter our minds and find solitude in God's presence. Aloneness is not a bad thing, but it's still an opportunity for the devil to leverage our isolation against us.

The deeper issue is not aloneness, but loneliness. Although closely related, there is actually a significant difference between the two. Aloneness is a state of being, but loneliness is a state of mind. It's a misnomer that being *alone* means being *lonely*. The reverse is also true. You can be lonely and surrounded by people.

Satan isn't partial to either form of aloneness. He's more interested in the symptoms of aloneness, such as boredom, lack of thought or disillusionment about life. The devil loves to play in the sandbox of mindless activity. He preys on those who are cursed with indecision and lead mechanical lives.

Whether you find yourself feeling lonely or just alone for the weekend, it's a vulnerable state that triggers temptation. You can't always avoid those desert seasons of life, but you can prepare yourself and know when to avoid sticky situations.

3. Lack

Have you ever given up something valuable in exchange for something that gives you immediate, but temporary gratification? Satan usually strikes at our weakest moments – when our minds are tired and our flesh is hungry. Samson was tempted with honey because he was hungry. When Jesus fasted forty days, the devil tempted Him to turn stones into bread.

The connection is obvious. Satan will always tempt you with something you lack or perceive as lack. The reason I say *perceive as lack* is because oftentimes, we crave things that we already have, but have lost interest or sight of it.

When you're fasting like Jesus, the temptation is quite literal. Someone walks by with a hamburger and your stomach growls and your mouth salivates. Then a voice says, "Just eat a small snack. Not a hamburger; that's going too far. But a granola bar is fine. It's kind of earthy and not very indulgent." You know what voice I'm talking about. However, life can leave us hungry in other ways besides food.

The lack of love can lead to a hungry heart – which aches for attention and acceptance. The lack of self-esteem can cause cravings for approval and a hyper-focus on physical appearance. When supply does not meet our demand, the tempter seizes the opportunity to exploit our desperation. But hunger itself is not the problem. God uses hunger to draw us closer to Him. Hunger can motivate and inspire people to reach for their dreams. The real problem is *misdirected* hunger.

When you're hungry, you must feed from the right source. Jesus could have turned stones into snacks, but instead He said: *"Man shall not live on bread alone, but on every word that comes from the mouth of God"* (Matt. 4:4). This was a temptation to elevate physical desire above spiritual need.

The devil was basically saying, "You only live once (YOLO). Enjoy the moment. Don't worry about the consequences. If it feels good, do it." But Jesus didn't take the bait. Had Jesus actually turned those stones into bread, imagine how delicious they would have been. That would have been the original Angel food cake! Instead, Jesus gave us a template to follow. He turned down the offer, making it clear that spiritual needs cannot be satisfied with physical things.

The enemy doesn't play fair. If he notices that you're confused, heartbroken or disenchanted with life, he'll waste no time to attack. The more weak and impulsive you are, the more likely he is to tempt you. Ask Esau, who traded his birthright for a bowl of bean soup (Gen. 25:29-34).

What a rip-off! When Esau exchanged the long-term benefits of his birthright for the temporary pleasure of food, he leaned entirely on his feelings. He was guided by impulse rather than wisdom. The devil hopes you make the same mistake. He hopes you take the bait in a moment of weakness, that you're driven by immediate desire.

My Own Worst Enemy

Your enemy is closer than you think. In fact, the enemy is wearing your clothes, using your toothbrush, driving your car, and carrying your wallet. Don't panic or call 9-1-1. The enemy I'm referring to is not an intruder.

The enemy is *you*.

The devil is not the only tempter you have to face. Some temptations come from within. The Bible states: *"When tempted, no one should say, 'God is tempting me.' For God cannot be tempted by evil, nor does he tempt anyone; each person is tempted when they are dragged away by their own evil desire and enticed. Then, after desire has conceived, it gives birth to sin; and sin, when it is full-grown, gives birth to death"* (James 1:13-15). Although we like to blame the devil for everything, scripture reveals the hidden monster lurking deep within all of us.

James uses the expression "dragged away by their own desire," which suggests that we are baited and hunted by our own lusts. To put it bluntly, the lying lion lies within. The apostle Paul also described this internal conflict: *"For the flesh desires what is contrary to the Spirit, and the Spirit what is contrary to the flesh. They are in conflict with each other, so that you are not to do whatever you want"* (Galatians 5:17).

If you're like me, maybe you're wondering, *what am I supposed to do?* If an enemy is on the outside *and* inside, where do you go? If you can't trust the devil (since he's a liar) and you can't trust yourself, who can you trust? Consider what Paul said prior to the verse above: "*...walk by the Spirit, and you will not gratify the desires of the flesh"* (v.16).

We cannot rely on ourselves to overcome temptation. Instead, we must depend on the Holy Spirit. Jesus taught us to pray: *"lead us not into temptation, but deliver us from the evil one"* (Matthew 6:13). This verse expresses our need to be led by the Spirit of God, not our feelings. In other words, don't try this on your own. You need God's help!

God is able to deliver you from the traps of the lying lion, and even those lurking lions from within.

In the next chapter, we will unpack an idea that I touched on briefly in this chapter, which is the danger of riding spiritual highs. You must resist the urge to settle for yesterday's blessing. If not, you may find yourself eating the lion's honey.

4

Canceled Fights

The Consequences of Giving Up

Samson faced the same lion twice. Yet the two episodes couldn't have been more opposite. The first match-up was an epic showdown of man vs. beast, and Samson won that round outright. He clobbered that bloodthirsty lion like nobody's business. It was a certified beat-down, a showcase in lion-killing without any special effects or stunt doubles.

The lion wasn't just knocked out, but was gruesomely ripped apart.

But the rematch was a different story. As I described in chapter one, the same lion that Samson tore apart in the first round, silently won in the second.

What happened here? How could someone with God-given power and an undefeated record completely fold? Well, I suggest that Samson lost this second match-up by making a crucial mistake. Rather than fight a new lion or a fresh opponent, he chose to relish in the past. Samson basically went back to polish his trophy, to relive the moment and maybe pat himself on the back.

Please consider the following principle: yesterday's victory *does not* guarantee tomorrow's victory. As believers, we cannot settle for past victories and recycled experiences. Yesterday's blessing was good for yesterday. But God wants to display His power in your life today!

Some biblical scholars believe that Samson was not very muscular, which conflicts with the usual perception we have of him. I always pictured Samson like those guys on the cover of Muscle & Fitness Magazine – a buff and toned specimen of a man. But this theory of a normal built man actually makes sense, because his enemies couldn't figure out how he was so strong.

If Samson had the physique of a body-builder, his source of strength would seem obvious.

Samson wasn't chosen because of his biceps. God picked him because He wanted to demonstrate His power through an ordinary human and receive every ounce of glory.

Samson was born for battle. He was made to be a fighter. God raised him up for great exploits, to lead and defend the Israelites with extraordinary strength. Samson was most effective, true to himself, when he was doing damage to the enemy.

When Fighters Won't Fight

You have been called to fight. Like Samson, you were not chosen based on your natural abilities or strength. God chose you based on His sovereign purpose. He specializes in using ordinary people for extraordinary purposes, so that He alone receives all glory. However, none of that matters if you cancel the fight.

I'm reminded of a pitiful moment in Israel's history where they looked like fighters, but refused to fight. The scene is recalled in Psalm 78:9: *"The children of Ephraim, being armed and carrying bows, turned back in the day of battle."*

The tribe of Ephraim was equipped and dressed for battle. Their armor was polished. Their arrows were freshly sharpened. Their troops were synchronized. Their equipment was reliable. These guys were armed and dangerous – fully loaded with plenty of backup. This wasn't just a training exercise or another military drill. The text implies that a real enemy was approaching. The situation was for real. It was time to launch the arrows and charge full-steam ahead.

Sounds great, right?

I wish I could report that what happened next was an all-out battle, resulting in a vigorous victory for God's people. Regrettably, the fight got canceled – not by the enemy and certainly not by God. Ephraim, the heavily favored champion, canceled the fight at the last minute.

It's one thing to fight and lose, to swing and miss – but to forfeit the fight without stepping onto the battlefield? That makes no sense.

How could an army of refined soldiers carrying advanced weapons just wimp out like that? Why didn't they break forth into battle and fulfill their destiny? What caused them to backtrack into mediocrity?

Several clues surface in verses 10 and 11: *"They did not keep the covenant of God; they refused to walk in His law, and forgot His works and His wonders that He had shown them."* After reading this text, we can identify three dysfunctions that caused Ephraim to cancel the fight. I would suggest that if you're not careful, you could find yourself in the same condition.

1. Broken Relationship

The scripture says that Ephraim "did not keep the covenant of God." The word "covenant" is a relationship term signifying a formal bond between two parties. A modern-day example of a covenant would be marriage – a lifelong commitment between a man and a woman. Apparently, Ephraim had drifted away from God and became enthralled with something else.

We don't know the specifics, but usually this language in scripture hints to idolatry – the worship of false gods. Idols were a habitual problem for the Israelites. Surrounded by cultures with visible gods and pagan images, they struggled to stay focused on their invisible God. Whenever the Israelites broke their covenant with God, He would lift his protective hedge and allow their enemies to rise up and oppress them. Then eventually, Israel would come to its senses and cry out for deliverance. This pattern of sin was a broken record, a repeated playlist in Israel's long and complicated history.

All God ever wanted was a monogamous relationship with His beloved people. His desire hasn't changed. He still wants to be known and loved by His people. He still requires that we place no other gods before Him — even idols like greed, lust and pride. The tribe of Ephraim broke their relationship with God, and in doing so, broke His heart.

Here's a simple question: do you have a personal relationship with Jesus Christ?

If you do, it would resemble your relationship with your spouse, if you're married. You would spend time together (prayer). You would learn about each other (read the Bible). You would make sacrifices for each other (worship). You would conduct yourself like a married person (holy living). You would start a family together (evangelism and spiritual fruit).

I'm perplexed when Christians claim to have a relationship with Jesus simply because they attend church.

Aside from owning a Bible, knowing Christian songs and attending church, how much of your life, your affections and desires are truly aligned with God's heart? If your relationship with Jesus is superficial or unclear, you may likely end up like Ephraim and cancel your fight – your destiny.

Okay, now I'm going to sound like a preacher.

Too many fights are canceled before they're ever fought, because our hearts are no longer tethered to the King's agenda. In general, we've become so self-absorbed and romanced by our own popularity that we've lost the motivation for anything that doesn't make us more comfortable or fit our fancy. But a heart that is truly tethered in covenant relationship with Christ will fight for what's right, not for what's convenient. You will submerge your desires in the flow of His desires – loving what He loves, rejecting what He rejects.

Your love story with God is not all rose pedals and poems. He's also calling you to rise up and fight for your faith and resist the temptation to marry the seductive beliefs of this world.

Don't break up with God over the flirtations of moral compromise and cheap grace. Throw yourself further into His arms. Leave the lifejacket on the shore and dive deeper into His love.

Let's not forget about Samson. I mentioned in chapter one that he broke his Nazarite covenant the moment he touched the lion's carcass. It seems that although the Spirit stirred *him*, he never stirred *the Spirit*. A heavenly gaze was missing from his eyes. Unlike the psalmist David (another lion killer) who was enthralled in the wonder of God, Samson didn't seem to relate with his power source. In fact, his only recorded prayer came at the end of his life when he asked for revenge against the Philistines (see Judges 16:28).

2. Broken Rules

Ephraim's second dysfunction was that "they refused to walk in His law." This isn't a big surprise. Why would a generation who broke their covenant with God still obey His rules? At this stage, the rules didn't matter anymore. They were living on their own terms, doing whatever seemed right in their eyes. This misadventure in moral relativism deepened their disbelief in God, causing them to question the purpose of the fight entirely. You could almost hear the soldiers saying to one another, "What's the point? Why shed any blood for a cause we don't believe in? Let's all calm down for a moment, think it through and weigh out the pros and cons. Do we really *want* this fight? Can't we just compromise a little or make a peace treaty where everybody wins?"

There is a similarity between the Tribe of Ephraim and Samson. Both parties knew God's commands, but they just didn't care anymore. Ephraim didn't "obey," implying they knew the laws and could not plead ignorance. They simply chose not to follow the rules. Samson had no excuse either. Due to his strict Nazarite vow, he was forbidden to touch anything unclean — specifically dead things. He had to have known that the lion's honey was off limits. Because of his holy calling, Samson would have been educated in the finer points of God's laws.

There's a well-known saying that "rules are made to be broken." The attitude behind such statements is obvious: most people don't like rules. They annoy us. They hinder us. It's true that we innately resist rules and constantly question *why* we need to follow them. But let's get something straight. Rules, whether man-made or biblical, don't benefit the ruler maker, but the rule keeper. Let me explain. The rules or commands in scripture are not necessarily for God's benefit, but for ours. Rules protect us because they anticipate behavior that could either harm others or ourselves.

We have road rules and laws that don't really benefit the government (unless you're fined), but are in place to benefit you. When your signal light turns green, you hope crossing traffic will stop at their red light. If not, there could be chaos and a serious accident. But what if a driver were to say, "I don't like rules, especially these man-made ones. They limit me and bother me. I'm driving forward whether it's red or green because I feel good about it."

As a parent, I have certain rules for my children to follow. Some rules I impose based on the Word of God, such as "don't lie." Others I impose are based on common sense and my own experiences, such as "don't play on the stairs." Both kinds of rules are mainly for my children's benefit, not mine.

Here's the thing, they don't like any of them. But they still need to obey them for their own good.

Covenant brings convictions, and convictions are worth defending. Ephraim's ambiguity towards God's law caused hesitation on the battlefield. They forgot what they stood for. That same kind of ambiguity in your life can leave you stuck in the locker room, instead of in the ring, fighting for your family or destiny. Personally, I can't keep quiet and watch marriages fall apart, young people lose their identity, long-standing values get trashed and leaders compromise their principles simply because it's more convenient. Stand for something. Fight for what's right.

3. Broken Remembrance

The Bible says Ephraim "forgot His works and His wonders that He had shown them." As their relationship with God faltered and rules were tossed out, their memory of His power slipped away. The people of Ephraim suffered from a case of spiritual amnesia, a condition that many believers are prone to. As life becomes hectic and problems pile up, we tend to forget about God and what He's done for us.

Spiritual amnesia creeps in those moments when we feel overwhelmed or afraid. Maybe after you bought your house or new car, your hours got cut at work. Maybe your health is declining just as insurance premiums are climbing. Maybe your friends are flaking out when you need a friend the most. If you're trying something new, maybe your past keeps getting thrown in your face. Perhaps you're dealing with the aftermath of a painful sin or personal failure. In other words, maybe you already touched the lion's honey of temptation.

Whether you're faced with one giant problem or a messy pile up of smaller issues – it's in that space of life that we tend to forget how mighty and merciful God is. Could this be why the Bible constantly reminds us to remember? Here are some examples:

- Remember the Sabbath day, to keep it holy (Ex. 20:8).
- Remember that the Lord your God led you on the entire journey these forty years (Deut. 8:2).
- Remember that you were a slave in the land of Egypt and the Lord your God redeemed you (Duet. 15:15).

- Remember what Moses, the Lord's servant commended you (Josh. 1:13).
- Remember His covenant forever – the promise He ordained for a thousand generations (1 Chron. 16:15).
- I will remember the deeds of the LORD; yes, I will remember your miracles of long ago (Psalm 77:11).
- Remember your Creator in the days of your youth (Eccl. 12:1).
- And he took bread, gave thanks and broke it, and gave it to them, saying, "This is my body given for you; do this in remembrance of me" (Luke 22:19).

God is not calling us to relive the past, but to remember it. Reliving the past would deny us the opportunity of the present. But remembering the past would secure our faith during turbulent times. Hebrews 13:8 reveals, *"Jesus Christ is the same yesterday and today and forever."*

Realizing that Jesus is the same "yesterday" in our memory, anchors the belief that He won't change today or tomorrow – no matter how bad it looks. If God did miracles before, He can do it again. If He blessed you before, He can bless you again. God's history in your life should encourage you to trust Him. Don't settle for yesterday's blessing, but let it motivate you to see greater things.

Ephraim's forgetfulness cost them a victory.

How about you? Has spiritual amnesia kept you from fighting and winning life's most important battles?

Fight the Good Fight

Paul encouraged Timothy to *"fight the good fight of the faith"* (1 Tim. 6:12). Notice he didn't say "fight the fight," which would assume *any* and *all* fights. Paul focused on the "good" fight, because not all fights are worth fighting.

This may sound like a contradiction to what I wrote earlier in this chapter, but hear me out.

Not all fights are created equal. If you fought every single fight in your view, you would eventually collapse or be overtaken. There's only so much one person can take. The key is to focus on the "good" fight, the worthy fight.

Some people are tenacious fighters, but caught in the wrong battle. They fight hard, but for the wrong reasons and against the wrong opponents. You must learn to pick your battles wisely because some fights have no trophies, no merit, and no other purpose but to distract you from your destiny. As a rule, I only fight when there's something worth fighting for, when there's something precious to gain or lose. If the basis of the fight is about proving a point, getting revenge or making yourself look better, it's time to walk away. It's better to have a bruised ego then a bruised life.

Occasionally, you might find yourself in a false fight. But when there's something worth fighting for, don't turn back.

Fight for your future.

Fight for your marriage.

Fight for your children.

Fight for your health.

Fight for the faith.

Fight for the salvation of others.

Fight for those who can't fight for themselves.

Don't squabble over silly things, trivial things, or temporal things. Stay focused on the *good* fight. Be a champion for good, a voice for virtue and justice, a defender for the defenseless, and a soldier for the gospel of peace. My heart breaks when I see Christians fighting other Christians, churches against churches, members against pastors. It's time to quit the infighting and focus on storming the gates of hell and reclaim every soul and family member it has stolen.

Canceled fights come with a high price. In the next chapter, this concept will crystalize through the life of King David – a man whose provocative drama of temptation and sin still shock us today. His moral downfall started with one critical decision – a decision not to fight.

5

Purge the Urge

Strategies for Personal Purity

There many examples to use when discussing the issue of temptation. But one that especially comes to mind is the story of David's affair with Bathsheba. Arguably the cause of David's greatest downfall, I think this example is worth learning from. This infamous affair came at a time when David was practically untouchable. His popularity was soaring and his name was synonymous with greatness. He had finally "arrived," so to speak – which makes his story of temptation even more compelling.

With all the temptation, immorality, murder and cover-ups, this definitely qualifies as the Rated-R part of the Bible.

Imagine if Twitter and Facebook existed during King David's time? The news of his affair and murder would have crashed the Internet with tweets, updates, and comments. All of the cable news networks would have had 24-hour coverage and special guest interviews lined up. This would have been a media circus. And yet, for those caught in the middle of this scandal, the pain and drama became unbearable.

When Kings Stay Home

I once read about how an Eskimo kills a wolf: He will repeatedly coat a blade in blood, allowing it to freeze, until the blade is completed covered. Then, he will place the knife in the snow. As the wolf licks the blood, his tongue is numbed, and his hunger is fueled. The wolf will lick the knife, cut his own tongue, and eventually bleed to death—all out of his own lust.

Likewise, Satan attempts the same strategy.

He hides sin with temptation (honey in a lion), and in our own appetite and lust, we destroy ourselves. Such was the case with David. Read what happened below:

"In the spring, at the time when kings go off to war, David sent Joab out with the king's men and the whole Israelite army. They destroyed the Ammonites and besieged Rabbah. But David remained in Jerusalem. One evening, David got up from his bed and walked around on the roof of the palace. From the roof he saw a woman bathing. The woman was very beautiful, and David sent someone to find out about her. The man said, "She is Bathsheba, the daughter of Eliam and the wife of Uriah the Hittite." Then David sent messengers to get her. She came to him, and he slept with her. (Now she was purifying herself from her monthly uncleanness.) Then she went back home. The woman conceived and sent word to David, saying, "I am pregnant" (2 Samuel 11:1-5).

Most of us know David as a giant killer, a musician, an anointed king, and a man after God's own heart. However, David's success made him spiritually lazy. At the time when kings would go out to fight, David stayed back. Instead of fighting, he reclined at home.

We're living in a time when war is being waged against the home, against family values, against morality, and against God's truth. Now more than ever, it's time for the church to come out swinging — not against people — against evil and sin.

The fight is on our front porch and ringing our doorbell. I'm calling on every believer, every father and mother, every young adult, to take a stand and refuse to kneel at the altar of society's status quo. A clarion call has been sounded for all of God's people to grab their swords, strap on their helmets, and take the enemy by the throat.

It's battle time. We cannot abandon our posts or simply play church.

As we investigate David's affair with Bathsheba, we have to understand how he let down his guard. Sure, he committed adultery. But sin doesn't exist in a vacuum. Certain behaviors and decisions make room for the enemy to attack. That's why scripture teaches us to "neither give place to the devil." We actually have the power to give or take away the devil's place to operate in our lives.

Through our conduct and thinking, we can give him a big sandbox to play around in. Let's look at what factors contributed to David's sin.

1. Negligence

In a previous time in David's life, he had killed 700 charioteers and 40,000 horsemen. Plus, he personally killed the commander of the Syrian army. One could argue that he was still riding the wave of his last accomplishment. Perhaps he became a little too comfortable, which led to negligence.

David belonged on the battlefield, fighting in the name of the Lord. He belonged with his troops, leading them to victory. But he stayed home. This was the beginning of his plight. From that point on, it was a downward spiral of mistakes and regrets. David was out of his element. He had a calling, but took an unnecessary day off. He had a duty to take charge in battle, but he let down his guard.

Negligence is simply carelessness to one's duty or responsibility. David neglected his duty by hiding in the palace. He neglected his role as king. He canceled his fight.

When you start neglecting your prayer life, your praise and worship, or your study of God's Word, you open a wider window for Satan to attack. On the contrary, the more you devote to prayer, worship and God's Word, the better you will be able to counter-attack the enemy.

Ephesians 4:27 warns, *"Neither give place to the devil."* Let's not give the enemy an inch to work.

2. Idleness

Negligence leads to idleness. As a kid, I remember hearing a preacher say, "An idle mind is the devil's workshop!" And honestly, it's still true. An idle life is the perfect place for the devil to set up his workstation.

What exactly is an idle life?

An idle life is one that is cursed with inaction, indifference, and driven by convenience. An idle person is passive and content with yesterday's strength.

Idle minds are virtually defenseless. When I think of the mind, I picture a bank building. If this bank were idle, it would have few, if any, security officers. Its cameras would be outdated or inoperable. Its alarm system might be functional, but lacking hi-tech tools such as sound and motion detectors. With an inactive security system, a bank becomes a prime target for robbery.

We can spiritualize this idea. If your mind is spiritually alert, it is sharper than an HD camera. The Holy Spirit is active and bears His badge of authority. Your purity alarm yearns for godly things, and there's no room for sin.

When we talk about David and Bathsheba, it is typically Bathsheba who gets the bad rap. We usually criticize her for bathing out in the open. But I believe the real responsibility falls on David. You can't convince me for one moment that David didn't know what he *might* see when he went on that roof.

David built that palace. He knew the palace like the back of his hand. There wasn't a spot that he didn't know about. When he went on that roof, he knew exactly where he was going. He didn't just stumble upon it. At evening time, David purposefully walked out on the roof.

After seeing Bathsheba bathing, his interest was sparked even further. At this point, David was about to cross the line.

Satan's *Man*hunt

For the remainder of this chapter, I'm going to address some men's issues. If you're a woman reading this, you're free to continue reading because it will help you better understand and protect your husband or sons. The Holy Spirit is leading me to share some raw and untamed advice for men who want to honor God and their families.

Standing on the roof of his palace, David made the decision to pursue a married woman. David saw, he understood the matter, and he made his move. He was much like Adam who saw the fruit, understood its danger, and took it anyway. Sin has consequences. It causes a ripple effect that affects not only you, but generations to follow.

Sexuality is out of control in our society. It has been the source of so much pain and heartache. It has split up families, wrecked marriages, and ruined communities. A man doesn't even have to leave the comfort of his home to find a secret source of pleasure. What used to be available only in rundown liquor stores and nightclubs can be accessed now on smartphones and computers.

I'm concerned about the growing rate of Internet porn sites, and the inconceivable growth in the numbers of men logging on to take a look. The sexualization of our culture has left men struggling to find some escape and peace of mind. Internet porn has reached epidemic proportions, luring in every type of man: fathers, husbands, grandfathers, businessmen, students, and even minsters.

Thousands upon thousands of pornographic websites are easily accessible and can be viewed anywhere with an Internet connection.

If you have dabbled with this issue or are fully engulfed, I'm not trying to judge you. That's our biggest error. We need to understand the problem before we start labeling. This subject is still highly taboo in many churches. But we must break down the walls and talk about a problem that is ruining lives by the minute.

For countless married men, the computer has become a ball and chain, shackling their joy and robbing them from real intimacy. Late at night, or right in the middle of the day, men are surfing right into a tidal wave of trouble. A great deal of the Internet has become nothing more than a lust lounge for men, and even women, to fulfill their empty fantasies. It's a dangerous addiction.

I understand that just the mention of this subject makes many feel uncomfortable. But we cannot end the discussion based on how we feel about it. If you're dealing with this issue, you can overcome it. Besides, it isn't only an Internet problem. Sexual temptation exists in a variety of forms: internet, print, television, and in person. The world isn't helping men much, either. With women wearing less and less, it's nearly impossible to escape. But you can overcome the temptations that lurk.

Here are four keys that will help you purge the urge and defeat sexual temptation.

1. Transparency

Failure to acknowledge the problem will result in failure to overcome it. If you're losing the battle with sexual temptation, stop the denial. It isn't just a little habit. And the argument that *"all men look"* has officially been thrown out. That's the oldest lie in the book. It's just an excuse.

You have to start telling yourself the truth. And no amount of truth will change you until you face reality. When you admit something isn't right, you can start traveling down the road to freedom. The hardest thing for men to admit is that there's a problem. We struggle with this idea. But for the sake of your spiritual and emotional health, you must come clean.

Without admitting the problem, one cannot repent. And repentance is necessary to move forward into God's blessings.

2. Responsibility

Never blame others for your actions. Sin always has a way of shifting the blame on someone else. Adam did this when he sinned. He blamed his wife Eve for his own failure. Even if other factors pushed you to the point of sinning, you must own your part. Adam thought he had reason to shift fault to Eve because she had pushed him to the edge. But Adam was his own man. He made his own decision. Likewise, you make your own decisions.

You must step up and take responsibility for your actions. Even if you feel it's an addiction, you still must own-up to your part.

3. Accountability

Make yourself accountable to spiritual authority. This can be a pastor, a mature believer or a seasoned mentor. Every man needs someone to whom he can bare his struggles and not be condemned. James 5:16 says, *"Therefore, confess your sins to one another and pray for one another, so that you may be healed. The effective prayer of a righteous man can accomplish much."*

Our instinct is to hide when faced with this sort of issue. Afraid of scrutiny, men conceal such matters and secretly war within themselves until they ultimately collapse.

Besides your boss at work, who do you report to? Who's holding you accountable? You need an authority figure that speaks truth and walks the talk. Don't pick a buddy who isn't strong himself.

Get under a man with authentic Christian faith and strong values. Our problem sometimes is that we're renegades and lone rangers, answering to no one and making up our own rules. But having an authority figure in your life will help you stay on track and keep you honest.

4. Spiritual Action

Develop a stronger relationship with God by spending time in His Word and presence. God's Word is powerful and relevant for daily life. It will help you root out the lustful desires and impulses.

Fuse the Word of God with daily prayer, and you will discover a life full of joy and power. Prayer is the source of strength and direction. Seek God in the morning, and you won't have trouble finding Him the rest of the day. Seek Him while He may be found. Ask Him to lead you away from temptation and to order your steps in righteousness.

5. Resistance

Lastly, learn to resist temptation and the bait that Satan uses against you. Resist the devil and he will flee. The effectiveness of this key really depends on whether you apply the prior ones: transparency, responsibility, accountability, and spirituality. All of this is possible through the power of the Holy Spirit. Don't be afraid or feel like you're fighting alone. God is with you – to strengthen you and hold you up.

If you can learn how to resist, you can live free of sexual impurity. No one shows us how to resist and defeat temptation quite like Joseph. His encounter with Potiphar's wife shows us exactly what to do when faced with sexual temptation.

Passing the Purity Test

Unlike David, Joseph teaches us not just about resisting temptation, but about living without compromise. Joseph, as many know, was the dreamer who saw himself becoming a prince with power.

Having older brothers who despised and sold him into slavery at a tender age, Joseph found himself taken to the foreign land of Egypt. It was there that Joseph served in the home of Potiphar.

Potiphar was an affluent man and a hotshot leader in Pharaoh's kingdom, with a very prestigious position. Joseph served in a great house with multiple levels of management and service. Favored of God, Joseph quickly found favor in Potiphar's eyes and was given charge over all of Potiphar's possessions. It wasn't long until Joseph was considered and respected as a leader in that house. Through God's goodness and grace, Joseph reached heights no one would have ever imagined—certainly not his brothers who so hatefully discarded him.

This goes to show that no matter what kind of situation you're thrown into, you can have success. No situation, no matter how messed-up, can keep you from becoming the person God created you to be. Joseph's kingly ambitions and extreme reverence for God promoted him into high places. He had God's favor upon him. He was successful.

Remember that David was also quite successful and highly respected in the kingdom when he was tempted and fell into sin with Bathsheba. But Joseph kept God close to his heart and vowed to live above mediocrity. His relationship with God was well-founded and deeply rooted. He honored God in every way he could. Even after rejection by his own flesh and blood, he continued to please God. Joseph lived in a way that brought honor to God and victory over temptation.

I'd love to share the whole life of Joseph in detail. It's so compelling. But for the purpose of dealing with temptation, I want to point out how he managed his situation with Potiphar's wife (read Genesis 39:6-15).

Joseph was caught in the wrong place at the wrong time.

Potiphar's wife was literally throwing herself at him, pressuring and seducing. Talk about persistent! This woman couldn't rest until she had Joseph. He was well-built and handsome. But I honestly don't believe that it was Joseph's physique that attracted this spiteful woman. It was his innocence, integrity, and uprightness that triggered her desire for him. It wasn't merely sex that she wanted.

She wanted to destroy him.

The enemy will always try to destroy the presence of holiness. The enemy will always attempt to sabotage God's chosen holy men. Just as in the account of Samson and Delilah, there is an evil spirit that specializes in attacking men who uphold a standard. Potiphar's wife represents a spirit that hates holiness and moral purity, especially in men. The following are some quick truths about Joseph that allowed him to resist temptation.

1. State your faith

The Bible says that Potiphar realized that the Lord was with Joseph. He was not shy about his relationship with God. He didn't broadcast it. He didn't announce it or distribute fliers to promote his ministry. People knew Joseph was a man of God by the way he lived. I'm sure he wasn't ashamed to speak about God, especially since interpreting dreams was one of his gifts. But his lifestyle spoke more than anything else about him.

2. Stay active

Unlike David, who became idle and hid in the palace, Joseph was busy working, planning, collaborating, managing duties, and serving in high capacities. He didn't have time to sit back. He was en route to his destiny. He was actively involved in the business of his life. Joseph's sense of purpose kept him focused and alert. It's when you stray away from your purpose that you begin to lose focus.

When you don't have something to fight for, you have nothing to live for. David got into trouble when he hid from fighting at the time when kings were supposed to fight. Don't lose your fight!

3. Set boundaries

Joseph understood and respected his boundaries. When he promoted Joseph, Potiphar made his guidelines clear. Joseph had rights to everything in Potiphar's house, except his wife. Solid lines were drawn, and Joseph knew them well. Let me ask you a few questions:

- Do you know your boundaries?
- Have you drawn clear moral lines?
- Do you know when or if you've crossed the lines?

Undefined boundaries create gray areas. It makes it easy to justify many things. When there are no solid boundaries about sin, it's easier to remain neutral and unchallenged. We all need to establish real-life boundaries.

For instance, if you know that certain sexually explicit magazines are positioned on an aisle of the grocery store, avoid walking down that aisle. If there's a TV channel known for racy and sensual material, don't even bother to see what's on that channel. Better yet, don't channel surf just to see if the coast is clear. Chances are, something is going to pop up and the images will be difficult to scrape from your mind. If there is a certain atmosphere or social scene that tempts you, don't go there.

We live in a world where morality has been blurred and people are calling "sin" something else. Joseph called sin what it was. He told Potiphar's wife, "How could I ever do such a wicked thing? It would be a great sin against God." We have to call it what it is.

Sin is sin.

There is no gray area. There is no middle ground. This understanding helped Joseph to resist temptation, and it will help you too.

6

Who Do You Think You Are?

Unlocking your True Identity

Within hours of hearing "This is my Son, whom I love," Jesus heard the devil's catchphrase, "If you are the Son…" He was attempting to plant doubt in Jesus about who He was. Obviously, he failed. Jesus would not be rattled or distracted from His purpose. He was certain about himself. The voice from heaven affirmed Him deeply. Jesus knew who He was.

The question is: do you know who you are?

At its core, temptation is an attempt to demolish your image and divert your destiny. If the devil succeeds at confusing your identity, his schemes will likely prevail. The more insecure you are, the more disposed you become towards unhealthy and ungodly choices.

Many believers find themselves stuck between "This is my son" and "If you are the son," between confidence and self-doubt about who they are in Christ. Maybe that's where you are at today. Or maybe like me, sometimes you feel like His son and sometimes you don't. I simply mean that there are days when I don't "feel" spiritual or confident about my status with Christ.

Like many pastors, I tend to feel spiritually low on Mondays, the morning after my highest day of the week – Sunday. On Mondays and even Tuesdays, I can feel like a spiritual slacker, even though I haven't done anything to justify those feelings.

On those days, I'm at my weakest.

I tend to feel distant from God and my prayers feel forced or clumsy. Then comes the pressure to prove who I am – prove that I'm still anointed or smart. If I'm honest, some Mondays I just don't feel good enough.

Do you have days like that? Do you ever find yourself second-guessing your worth or position in Christ?

Do you have moments when you wonder if you're good enough, strong enough, or anointed enough?

Maybe there are days when the moment you step outside your house, you collide with the devil's catchphrase, "If you are the son." Maybe his catchphrase shows up at work or at school.

Maybe you're in the middle of a crisis and keep hearing "If you are a son or daughter of God, and He loves you...why are you going through this? Why are you hurting so bad or dealing with so much drama?"

I Am Who God Says I Am

One of the greatest questions you will ever ask is "Who Am I?" This question has baffled humanity for eons. Throughout time, mankind has been on an elusive quest to discover the meaning of life and who we are.

In ancient times, man gazed upward to the stars that freckled the night, hoping to connect the dots of his existence. During the Renaissance and Enlightenment eras, man began to look outward through the lenses of philosophy and science. This gave way to modern humanism, where man began to look inward to find himself and unlock the mystery of his identity.

I'm going to put it plainly. Only God can unlock the revelation of who you are. And there is nothing more powerful than living with the awareness of your God-given identity, the core of your being.

The devil's fiercest temptations are linked to insecurity. For example, even though God loves you unconditionally, if the devil convinces you that God doesn't love you, he will tempt you to earn God's love or find love in the wrong places. If the devil causes doubt about your self-worth, he will tempt you to draw unhealthy attention to yourself. If the enemy convinces you that you're not blessed, it will tempt you to prove you're "blessed" through materialism or false prosperity.

Jesus didn't have to turn stones into bread to prove He was God. He is God. You don't need to prove who you are; you just need to be who you are. Matthew 3:17 states: *"And a voice from heaven said, "This is my Son, whom I love; with him I am well pleased."* The same voice that affirmed Jesus at His baptism, is affirming you today.

I Am Accepted

When Jesus heard, "This is my Son," it was a divine confirmation of His position as the Son of God. For 30 years, Jesus knew that Joseph wasn't His real father. Even at twelve-years-old, He was "about his Father's business." But this is the first recorded mention where The Father called Him "my Son." If it was necessary for Jesus, God in flesh, to hear the words "my Son," how much more important is it for us? Jesus wouldn't launch his public ministry without hearing the voice of acceptance.

As humans, we crave acceptance. We are born with a throbbing desire to belong. It is what drives us internally. That is why a child, without being told or guided, will inherently seek the acceptance of his father or mother. Children want to know they have a place in the family. Nobody wants to be left out, overlooked or viewed as an outsider.

I recall an occasion when my five-year-old son, Makai caught me off guard. I think he was playing with his toys, and I was sitting at the kitchen table. Then out of nowhere he asked a question that baffled me.

"Daddy, am I still your son?"

My immediate thought was, "Huh?"

His question completely threw me off. But without much hesitation, I quickly replied, "Yes of course! You'll always be my son." If I'm being honest, the question broke my heart. I thought to myself, *what did I do to make my son ask this question?* Had I treated him any different? Had I said something that made him feel this way? I couldn't figure it out.

As soon as I replied, he just kept on playing. Ironically, he started his question by calling me "Daddy". He knew who I was. But something made him wonder if he was "my son."

I can't help but think how often we call the Lord our "Father," but don't feel like His son or daughter. I wonder if sometimes we just know His title as Father, intellectually or scripturally, but don't see ourselves as His children. Maybe you feel like your position in Christ is based on what you've done and what's been done to you. Perhaps, the devil has whispered "if you were *really* his child, you wouldn't be hurting like this, struggling this like, or messing up so much."

This truth needs to flood your heart: if you are His child, He will not unchild you. Your condition does not change your position.

You are accepted.

You belong to the Lord.

It only takes one voice of acceptance to silence a thousand echoes of rejection. Listen to the Holy Spirit speaking, "You are my son"..."You are my daughter." The title of "son or daughter" cannot be earned, but only embraced.

Knowing who you are is tethered to knowing *whose you are*. Paul wrote: *"If we live, we live for the Lord; and if we die, we die for the Lord. So, whether we live or die, we belong to the Lord" (Romans 14:8).* When you are born-again, your old nature is replaced with a new nature in Christ. You belong to Him. Stand tall in your acceptance.

I Am Beloved

The voice from heaven said, "this is my Son, whom I love." Other Bible translations read, "this is My beloved Son." Before Jesus held any miracle crusades or preached a sermon, He found a loving embrace with His Father. We must realize that God's love does not flow from the fountain of human effort, but divine favor. Ephesians 1:6 says, *"to the praise of the glory of His grace, by which He made us accepted in the Beloved."* Your beloved identity springs from God's grace. It cannot be earned.

John wrote, *"We love Him because He first loved us"* (1 John 4:19). This little verse says a lot. First, God's love precedes our love. He loved you before you loved Him, before you met Him, before you cleaned up your act and paid attention. He loved you at your worst, your lowest, your craziest, your darkest moments.

God loved you when you were most unlovable. Another truth is, God's love empowers our love. We love him "because" He loved us. You have been granted grace, the ability to love Him in return. Perhaps you already know that you're His beloved. But do you know how to "be loved" by Him?

It's unfortunate how many Christians strive to be loved by God, without realizing that He loves them the same yesterday, today, and tomorrow. His love doesn't fluctuate or increase as you get more spiritual. Nothing you do can make God love you more or less. Your beloved identity is not based your righteousness, but on Jesus' righteousness.

The good news of the gospel is that God *so loved* the world that He gave His only Son (ref John 3:16). God's belovedness towards you is based on *who* He is, not in *how* righteous you are.

The word is "be-loved," not "do-loved." Christians waste so much time jumping through hoops to win God's affection – instead of just resting in it. Can you "be loved" by the God who "so loved" you? Or, is your belovedness tangled up with strings of fear and doubt? When we falsely believe that His love is rooted in our performance, we feel loved when we succeed and rejected when we fail. Once we're convinced that He loves us less, the tendency is to disobey even more.

The root of disobedience is disaffection. But awakening to your belovedness in God should prompt a desire to obey Him. Maybe this is why Jesus said, *"If you love me, keep my commands"* (John 14:15). Love is the basis for obeying God's commands and resisting temptation. You shouldn't resist temptation solely because it's sinful or punishable, but because it offends the lover of your soul. Those who obey are those who realize that their status with God is not rooted in their flawed obedience to Christ, but in His righteousness.

Don't just acknowledge God's love. Soak it in. Bask in the depth of His delight in you – until every fiber in your being knows that you are His beloved. Your state of belovedness expresses the core truth about your existence. God didn't *need* to create you, He *wanted* to. Love was His motivation.

Maybe you're wondering what this has to do with temptation. It has everything to do with it. If the devil can get you to doubt your beloved identity, or convince you into trying to earn it, his temptations will prey on those insecurities. Jesus overcame temptation partly because He never stopped hearing, "you are my beloved Son." Listen closely, because the same voice is speaking to you today.

I Am Affirmed

Jesus also heard the voice from heaven say, "with Him I am well pleased." Again, these words were spoken *before* any demons were cast out, diseases healed or water turned into wine. The words "I am well pleased" were not celebrating Jesus' accomplishments, because He hadn't actually done anything yet. The Father was not delighting in Jesus' works, but in His existence.

I don't think the common believer lives with the daily awareness of God's delight over him. The majority of us know it's important to praise God, as the scriptures teach. But most of us don't know that God praises us, too. The idea that God *praises us* almost sounds blasphemous. But keep in mind; we're talking about praise, not worship. God doesn't worship us, but He does praise or cheer us on like a father in the bleachers. Here are scriptures that speak of God's praise or delight in us:

- He will take great delight in you; in his love he will no longer rebuke you, but will rejoice over you with singing (Zephaniah 3:17).
- He rescued me because he delighted in me (Psalm 18:19).
- The Lord delights in those who fear him (Psalm 147:11).
- Circumcision is circumcision of the heart, by the Spirit, not by the written code. Such a person's praise is not from other people, but from God (Romans 2:29).
- Therefore, judge nothing before the appointed time; wait until the Lord comes. He will bring to

light what is hidden in darkness and will expose the motives of the heart. At that time each will receive their praise from God (1 Corinthians 4:5).

An interesting fact about my family is that my two older brothers and I attended the same high school as my dad. In addition to that, we all played football. Some years ago the four of us took a picture with our lettermen jackets from Mount Pleasant High School. That famous family photo hangs proudly in my parents' home. It sort of captures the tradition of us Rodriguez boys and the game of football. My dad was a great athlete who set some amazing records in high school. Both of my older brothers were great athletes who exceled not only in football, but baseball and wrestling.

During my senior year, I was determined to keep the Rodriguez tradition and play football. But one thing became obvious for me – I wasn't very good. Sure, I made the team, wore a uniform and laced up my cleats. But aside from lining up for field goals or a random play at the tight-end position, I didn't see much playing time.

I never scored any touchdowns.

I didn't make any big plays.

My last name was even misspelled on my home jersey – "Rodriguz." I was probably the last person on the team who deserved any cheers.

But to my dad, that made no difference.

He showed up for every game and cheered me on as if I was the starting quarterback. Sometimes during games, I would glance up into the bleachers and see my parents and think… "I hope they're not disappointed if I don't play today." But I figured out that my dad didn't come to my games and cheer me on because I proved something on the field. He came and cheered because I'm his son – on and off the field, win or lose. His delight was to be there for me and with me. He praised me not for scoring, but for being his son.

God doesn't praise you for what you do, but for who you are. He raves about you simply because you are His child. He sings over your soul and smiles at your existence. The Christian life is so much more fun when you live *from* His affirmation, not *for* His affirmation. Your praise of God ricochets His praise of you.

Your affirmation is not based on your good works, but on the finished work of Jesus on the cross. This truth is the key to your deliverance from every war that rages from within. It is the secret to entering God's rest. When you feel bombarded by trials and temptations, remember that God overwhelms what overwhelms you.

God was pleased with you, before you did anything pleasing.

That should drive you to please Him more. This doesn't mean that your life was or is perfect, or that you were born sinless. But like a mother gazes upon her newborn baby with wrinkled skin, blemishes and birthmarks – He's pleased with your presence. God loves you like nobody else does, because you are a piece of Him – created in His image. It's time to start living like that truth is real and claim your beloved identity.

False Identities

The reason why most people are not happy with themselves is because they spend their lives posing as someone else. What a waste of time and energy! If you knew who God created you to be, you wouldn't desire to be anyone else. You have God's unique signature. Anything less is forgery.

The reality is, we tend to define ourselves based on the wrong things. Before I wrap up this chapter, allow me to briefly expose four false identities:

1. I am Double

This speaks of leading a double life. You're stuck in a contradiction with yourself. You're unable to define the role you should play because you're reading from two different scripts.

Social media allows you to be whoever you want to be. The only problem is, who you are online is not who you really are.

James 1:8 teaches that a "double-minded" person is unstable, confused about himself and can't decide who he wants to be. This confusion dissolves when you embrace the person God made you to be. It's better for people to hate who you really are, then to be in love with who they think you are. Who you really are is far more interesting then who you're pretending to be.

2. I am What I do

Many people define themselves by what they do, such as their career or ministry. If that's you, I would call you a "human doing," instead of a "human being." When you meet someone new, usually the first or second question you might ask is, "what do you do for a living?" Your occupation is the easiest way to describe yourself and make conversation. But building your identity solely on your work is a mistake. For instance, what happens if you lose your job or your title?

"Human doings" tend to be insecure and feel they have to earn their self-worth – or in spiritual terms, earn their salvation.

Ephesians 2:8-10 states, *"For by grace you have been saved through faith, and that not of yourselves; it is the gift of God, not of works, lest anyone should boast. For we are His workmanship, created in Christ Jesus for good works, which God prepared beforehand that we should walk in them."* According to this passage, we are not saved *by* works, but *for* works.

3. I am What I have

We are a society of status symbols. People want the flashy cars, high-end fashion and coolest gadgets. But allowing your possessions or checking account balance to define you will make you a slave to things. Possessions will possess you. Jesus said, *"For what profit is it to a man if he gains the whole world, and loses his own soul? Or what will a man give in exchange for his soul?"* (Matthew 16:26).

Don't base your identity on assets and possessions. Instead, let the precious blood of Jesus calculate your worth. Jesus bled and died on the cross for you. Your worth is not defined by your net-worth (which can change tomorrow), but on the unchangeable truth of God's love for you. I'll be addressing the issue of materialism in a later chapter.

4. I am My Problem

There are many who define themselves by their problems or perceived dysfunctions. I'm reminded of man named Bartimaeus whose sight was healed by Jesus. So often is he labeled "blind Bartimaeus." But notice what he did when Jesus called him: *"So Jesus stood still and commanded him to be called. Then they called the blind man, saying to him, "Be of good cheer. Rise, He is calling you." And throwing aside his garment, he rose and came to Jesus"* (Mark 10:49-50).

In biblical times, the sick and poor were stigmatized by their outer garments. Bartimaeus' garment was his identity. It said to society, "I'm blind" or "I'm dysfunctional." But when Jesus called him, He threw off his garment and essentially said "That's not me anymore. That's what I thought I was supposed to be." When Jesus calls your name, every false identity is exposed.

It's time to peel off every bad label that you've wearing and accept as your identity, such as…Failure, Addict, Victim or Loser. Temptations feast on the insecure and falsely identified. But in Jesus Name, you're going to walk in confidence – knowing how beloved and pleasing you are to God. You were created in His image. Maybe that's why the enemy hates you so much. Because when he sees you coming, he sees the reflection of God.

7

Untamed Emotions

Controlling your Feelings and Impulses

It feels good to feel good. Forgive me for simplifying that thought. But it's true. Satan wouldn't tempt us with pleasure unless it promises exactly what our flesh craves. Remember Samson? It's been a few chapters since I've mentioned him. I guess I cut him some slack. Well, now it's time to rummage a little deeper into his mistakes, because if anybody knows the temptation and downfall of pleasure, it's Samson. His ordeal with the lying lion was just the beginning of his slipups. The honey in the lion was no match for the honey named "Delilah."

A book about temptation wouldn't be complete without discussing this infamous affair. For as much as we've heard about Samson and Delilah, this provocative and disastrous saga still heats up the pages of the Bible. You can find the tragic details in Judges chapter 16.

Delilah was, to put it bluntly, a conniving woman who used her sexuality to manipulate and destroy Samson. We know she was from the valley of Sorek, but we're not told how or where these two "supposed" lovebirds met. Most scholars presume Delilah was fairly young, around 20 years old, and breathtakingly beautiful. Her runway model looks is probably what caught Samson's attention. But she wasn't his biggest problem.

Making Sense of our Senses

It could be argued that Samson's greatest flaw was that he was emotionally, not spiritually controlled. This seems a bit ironic. How could a man with such supernatural power be so helpless? The same guy who wiped-out a thousand Philistines with a donkey's jawbone was paralyzed by one woman with a pair of scissors.

Samson could shred his opponents. But he couldn't tame his own lust and anger. He failed to conquer the impulses of his flesh. Delilah was the devil's pawn, no question, but she only did what Samson allowed her to do. Samson's greatest enemy was not the Philistines or Delilah, but himself. His wild emotions got the best of him.

Emotional people are not necessarily those who cry about everything, but those whose decisions are informed more by their feelings, instead of wisdom. Emotional people are sensual people. We often associate sensuality with sex. But its meaning transcends that. The word "sensuality" implies a total focus on the pleasure of all five senses—touch, sound, sight, taste and hearing.

Samson's deeper issue was not his attraction to beautiful women, but his inability to control his senses, the impulses raging within himself. Sex wasn't Samson's only problem. He had other self-destructive patterns, like refusing counsel and having a short fuse. His fits of rage turned him into something like The Incredible Hulk, the green comic book character with uncontrolled anger and superhuman strength. That's a dangerous combination.

Our adversary loves to play puppet-master with our emotions – pulling and provoking negative reactions. But emotions are not your enemies. And they're also not your best friends. Emotions are triggered by either pleasure or pain, which means they can be positive or negative. In simple terms, emotions are like escalators – moving you up or down. But honestly, it's a little more complicated than that.

When negative emotions like depression or anger are left untamed, they will claw your mind. The devil knows this too. He is a professional at using your raw emotions against you and tempting you through your feelings.

God wants your emotions to be healthy. In 3 John 1:2 we read: *"Dear friend, I pray that you may enjoy good health and that all may go well with you, even as your soul is getting along well."* Your emotions reside in your soul. If your soul is not well, your life won't be well. No matter how much money you earn – if your soul is not well, your life will not be. No matter how many friends you have – if your soul is not well, again, your life will not be. No matter if you attend church, if your soul is not well, your life will reflect that.

See my point?

Your emotional health is the wellbeing of your life. Proverbs 4:23 says, *"Above all else, guard your heart, for everything you do flows from it."* The emotions of your heart and soul are veins that flow through every area of your life. This is why we must "guard" and tame our emotions when they roar. We all have at least one emotion or impulse that demands more taming than others.

For some, it's guilt or shame; for others its anger or envy. We all have impulsive tendencies or inclinations that need to be controlled. Easier said than done, right?

The tension between what you should do and shouldn't do, between impulse and self-control, is part of human nature and unavoidable. Listen to the apostle Paul confess the inner conflict he had with sinful impulses:

"For I do not do the good I want to do, but the evil I do not want to do — this I keep on doing. Now if I do what I do not want to do, it is no longer I who do it, but it is sin living in me that does it. So I find this law at work: Although I want to do good, evil is right there with me. For in my inner being I delight in God's law; but I see another law at work in me, waging war against the law of my mind and making me a prisoner of the law of sin at work within me. What a wretched man I am! Who will rescue me from this body that is subject to death? Thanks be to God, who delivers me through Jesus Christ our Lord!" (Romans 7:19-25)

Without dissecting this entire passage, I simply want to point out that the struggle is real. If a legendary apostle like Paul struggled to tame his impulses and emotions, we shouldn't be afraid to admit ours. Furthermore, we must recognize that until we die and go to heaven, the inner tug-of-war (Spirit vs. flesh) will be a constant reality.

Yet, there is still hope while we live on earth. Jesus Christ can deliver us from the curse of sin and rescue us when we find ourselves surrounded with temptations.

Emotional Slaves

Before the fall, Adam and Eve's emotions were perfectly balanced. They did not argue, they were not jealous, nor did they attempt to manipulate each other. God gave us emotions to enjoy His presence and creation. But after the fall, Adam blamed Eve, and they both became ashamed. They were now ambiguous towards God and each other. Emotions were suddenly untamed and darkened by the affects of sin. This complicated the world, even though the total population was only two.

Since the fall, we can now be victims of our moods – as they swing from one extreme to another. Instead of mastering our emotions and impulses, we become slaves to them. We live as if we are mere recipients of emotions. We say, "I *fell* in love" or, "He was *overcome* with guilt" or, "I was *caught* in the moment," as though we are powerless to rule our feelings.

I'm not saying all emotions are evil. Clearly, emotions such as love and joy are positive. The problem occurs when *destructive* emotions sway your behavior and form unhealthy attachments. It's okay to have raw and real emotions, so long as they don't guide your life. Listening to your emotions is one thing, but following them is another. Jesus had raw emotions, but they did not rule Him. He became angry, but never lost His temper. He was hurt by betrayal, but didn't become bitter. He sobbed with grief, but didn't drown in depression. Jesus kept His feelings in check. He was led by the Spirit and not by the flesh (feelings, emotions and moods).

We are emotional beings, but we don't have to be emotionally driven. Here is a list of questions to think about:

- Do I tend to overreact when someone makes a slightly hurtful comment?
- Am I anxious or moody?
- Do I easily lose my temper?
- Do I dwell on angry feelings, long after the incident?
- Do I give up when my mood darkens?
- Do I indulge in my impulses?
- Am I constantly finding fault with others or even myself?
- Do I often feel sorry for myself?

The worst kind of decisions are emotional decisions, choices we make based on how we feel in the moment. I speak from my own experiences when I say that emotional decisions rarely pane out into something positive. Usually, emotional decisions result in regret – where you think to yourself, "I should have known better." There's a price to pay for letting your emotions guide your decisions.

Perhaps you recall the story of when Isaac, who was blind, blessed his son Jacob (see Genesis 27). In order to steal his older brother's birthright, Jacob disguised himself as Esau. The Bible says Esau was a hairy guy, and Jacob had smooth skin. So with his mother's coaching, Jacob wrapped his hands with goat hair and put on his brother's clothes. This scheme was an attempt to trick Jacob's father into thinking he was Esau.

Their scheme worked.

When Jacob went to his father, he asked him to get closer so he could feel him. That's when things got weird. Jacob sounded like himself, but felt like Esau. This threw Isaac off. His senses were telling him two different stories. In that moment, Isaac depended on what he felt over what he heard. The wrong decision was made. Instead of giving the birthright to Esau, the rightful heir, he gave it to Jacob.

Isaac was betrayed by what he felt.

From a biblical standpoint, hearing (sound) always trumps feeling (touch). Scripture reveals, *"faith comes by hearing the Word of God"* (Romans 10:17) and *"Whoever has ears, let them hear what the Spirit says"* (Revelation 2:7).

But the concept of touch usually has a negative overtone. For example, Thomas was called a doubter because he needed to touch Jesus' nail-prints before he believed. The Bible contains many passages about what not to touch, and seldom does it give permission to touch. In a prior chapter, I mentioned Samson's Nazarite vow that banned him from touching anything dead.

Broken Walls

It concerns me how many Christians are guided more by feelings, rather then faith – more by emotions, then truth. I cringe when people say things like, "I don't feel God" or, "I feel like I've fallen out of love with my spouse." Friend, it doesn't matter what you feel or how you feel. In my opinion, feelings are so overrated. Take love for example. Love is not just a feeling – it's a choice.

Jesus said, "Love your neighbor." How are you supposed to feel compassion towards someone you don't even know? If you were to wait until you felt something before you "loved" your neighbor, you would never act in love. But when you respond to what you hear God saying in His Word, the feelings will follow.

Stop idolizing your emotions and start commanding them. Rule your feelings based on the truth of God's Word. You won't wake up every morning "feeling" saved or loved. But you must control your feelings by declaring truth. Emotional Christians require the highest maintenance in the Church. Because they can't control their feelings, they constantly have to be reminded of truths they should already know. They suck their thumbs when hurt, and thumb their noses when guilty of hurting others. It's time to get a grip on your emotions and let truth guide you.

Our emotions inform us of what's internal, but the Spirit informs us of what's eternal. Through the power of the Holy Spirit, you can tame your emotions and take charge. One of the nine fruits (virtues) of the Spirit is self-control, the power to restrain yourself from evil and indulgence (see Galatians 5:22-23). I find it interesting that self-control appears last on the list of fruit. We don't know if the apostle Paul listed the fruit in sequential order or randomly, but self-control serves as the capstone – probably because it takes a lot of self-control to exercise the other eight virtues.

The Greek word translated "self-control" is *egkrateia,* which is derived from two other Greek words — *en* and *kratos*. *En* means "in" and *kratos* means "strength" or "power." Based on the Greek root words, self-control implies *power within*. Don't get this confused with the human philosophy of willpower – an intellectual strength or "mind over matter." New Age humanism claims that everyone has a righteous, innate power source waiting to be tapped. But the apostle Paul taught: *"The mind governed by the flesh is hostile to God; it does not submit to God's law, nor can it do so"* (Romans 8:7).

Willpower cannot be trusted.

We need God's power to govern our will.

The English term "self-control" is a bit misleading. This spiritual virtue is not about "self" controlling "self" through mental toughness. It's about relying on the Holy Spirit to control your desires. God will not violate your free will to make choices. But if you allow Him to, He will enable you *"to will and to act according to His good purpose"* (Philippians 2:13). The key is to stay wrapped in God's belovedness towards you – to live in the power of the gospel.

Without self-control over our emotions and impulses, we become *"like a city whose walls are broken down"* (Proverbs 25:28). No self-control equals a defenseless heart and mind. And a defenseless heart resorts to heartless defenses. In other words, the more defenseless you are against your emotions and temptations, the crueler you become inside and out. Because of these broken walls, the enemy will raid your mind with jealous, angry or lustful thoughts, and then leave you hypersensitive to correction.

The Opposite of Self-Control

Self-control is not about becoming a control freak – which is a total contradiction. Control freaks are usually the most out of control. They can't even control their desire for control. Control freaks seek inner peace by trying to control everything and everyone else around them. Controlling external things, they feel "in control" and empowered. Ironically, I don't know one control freak that's actually happier and healthier because of their controlling behavior. It generally has the reverse effect – leaving you less patient and more impulsive.

The opposite of self-control is not necessarily self-indulgence. In many cases, indulgent or impulsive behavior is merely the symptom of deeper issues. Allow me to point out three factors that are linked to untamed emotions.

1. Fear

Control doesn't flow from the outside in, but from the inside out. One of my favorite New Testament verses is 2 Timothy 1:7, which states: *"For God has not given us a spirit of fear, but of power and of love and of a sound mind."* The phrase "sound mind" literally means "self-control" or "self-discipline." We are usually energized by the first two virtues – power and love.

Who doesn't want more power? Who would reject more love? We celebrate these qualities. But somehow, the spirit of a sound mind doesn't excite us as much.

Paul presented a contrast to fear by revealing its opposites – power, love and self-control. The opposite of self-control is not merely self-indulgence, but fear. When there's no self-control (or power and love), fear is the driving force for our behavior. Fear creates an urge to distract yourself from your deepest unmet needs by filling those voids with whatever form of pleasure that numbs your reality.

Many young women don't have sex with manipulative men just for the pleasure of it, but to cope with their fears of being alone or rejected. Many obese people don't overeat simply because food tastes so good, but to cope with insecurities or fears.

Don't get me wrong. Not every indulgence is a cry for help, but without God's power, every cry for help leads to indulgence.

2. Lack of hearing

I'm reminded of the unfortunate scene at Jesus' arrest in Gethsemane. Peter tried to intervene by cutting a man's ear off. This was no heroic action, but a rash distraction from Jesus' mission. Read for yourself in John 18:10-11: *"Then Simon Peter, having a sword, drew it and struck the high priest's servant, and cut off his right ear. The servant's name was Malchus. So Jesus said to Peter, 'Put your sword into the sheath. Shall I not drink the cup which My Father has given Me?'"* In contrast, the gospel of Luke tells us that Jesus healed and reattached the man's ear.

Peter reacted out of impulse, instead of discernment. His swift aggression, although appearing to be righteous, was an overreaction that wounded someone.

Impulsive people tend to speak or act first, before considering the damage they might cause. Feeling justified by their emotions, they hurt the wrong people for the wrong reasons. Impulsive people don't see how their actions impact others. Maybe I'm describing you. Maybe you're allowing your emotions to justify your actions.

Peter's impulsiveness cut off a man's ear. The spiritual lesson is that impulsiveness cuts off your ability to hear from God and perceive His will. As you lean more and more on your flesh (feelings), you deafen yourself to God's voice. The Bible says, *"He who has an ear, let him hear what the Spirit says to the churches..."* (Rev. 2:7). If you're always inclining towards your flesh, your impulses, you won't receive the wisdom and direction that the Holy Spirit gives.

3. Lack of vision

The Bible tells us, *"Where there is no prophetic vision the people cast off restraint"* (Proverbs 29:18, ESV). Another translation says, *"When there's no vision, the people get out of control."* Evidently, there's a link between the lack of divine guidance and the lack of self-control. Allow me to paraphrase this verse in my own language: "When you lack direction, you lack discipline."

Direction produces self-discipline, which then produces healthy decisions. Those with a habit of making bad decisions based on emotion or impulse usually have impaired vision for their future. When you have direction, it motivates you to make the right kind of choices.

If your direction (vision) is to finish college and earn your degree, then you'll make the necessary sacrifices in order to achieve that dream. There may be nights when you can't hang out with friends because you're studying for a test or writing a paper.

If your vision is to land a great job or start your own business, then it will require self-discipline to go the extra mile and put in the time. If your direction is to have a healthy and fit lifestyle, then you'll need self-control when ordering at the restaurant and discipline to exercise regularly. If you're planning to get married and want to be sexually pure on your wedding day, then it means controlling your urges and resisting temptation while you wait.

Your direction helps determine your disciplines.

The most out of control people are usually those with the least direction in their lives. Let's not forget about Samson, who embodied this reality. His lack of divine guidance put him in a compromising situation, which led to poor decision-making.

If direction produces discipline and self-control, where do we get direction? If you want direction, you start by knowing the Director – Jesus Christ. He taught us to pray, "do not lead us into temptation." Keep turning the pages and you'll discover how your prayer life plays a role in directing your steps and defeating your temptations.

8

When You Pray

Deepening your Conversations with Jesus

My prayer life has been a journey. I don't mean it in some hyper-spiritualized way, but in the most honest and real sense. As I look back over the course of my Apostolic experience, prayer has always been my most cherished and at times most difficult practice.

For some years, I pretended I knew how to pray. I developed the art of saying prayers, leading prayers and even teaching about prayer, but struggled to enjoy a guilt-free, fulfilling prayer life. Let's be honest, most Christians are afraid to open up about their real prayer lives. I think our fear of rejection or disapproval keeps us from admitting when our prayer life is stuck. Most teachings on prayer indirectly make us feel guilty from either not praying enough or incapable of measuring up. In my case, what ensued was an attempt to prove myself and please God with my prayers, instead of praying as a beloved and pleased son. I was praying *for* His acceptance, not *from* His acceptance. That makes a huge difference.

Prayer is much more enjoyable and relational when you pray from a position of acceptance and belovedness, rather than fear or condemnation.

Unlike prior chapters, I warn you that I will ramble on a bit more in this chapter. My thoughts on prayer tend to spray and not shoot. It's probably because I'm writing this book at a time when my own prayer life is undergoing a renovation of sorts. No, I'm not unveiling some non-biblical or mystical philosophy about prayer. Rather, I'm unpeeling the layers and rediscovering God's original design for prayer. So please excuse all the scaffolding around my thoughts. However, I promise, what you learn will change your life.

Prayer Mirrors the Gospel

We have to repair our broken images of prayer and understand our position in Christ. Knowing your position unlocks the possibility of knowing God more intimately, thus allowing Him to lead you into righteousness. But I'm not about to offer you another formula for prayer. Formulas aren't always bad. Sometimes they can help jumpstart your prayer life. But many of our formulas are flawed and unreasonable, and become yet another "thing to do" that leads to more frustration.

Instead, I hope to lead you into the rhythm of prayer where you realize that it's about intimacy with God, not a heavenly vending machine for what we want – or a religious substitute for grace.

Prayer mirrors how we understand and live the gospel. How we pray is a reflection of how we view God and ourselves. To say it another way, how you view Jesus and His gospel will express itself in the way you approach Him.

Therefore, prayer is both the daily and honest application of the gospel in our lives. Proclaiming, serving and loving are also applications of the gospel, but cannot be demonstrated in solitude since they flow outwardly.

Our prayer lives don't reveal how spiritual we are, but how *gospeled* we are.

Conversely, the most prayerful are not always the most spiritual, but the spiritual are always prayerful. I know people who supposedly pray a lot, and years later are still unfruitful and stagnant. Perhaps because it's not entirely about what or how often you pray, but *how* you pray. In prayer there is little virtue in saying the right things, and far greater virtue in believing the right things – about God and yourself.

Jesus taught, *"When you pray, do not use vain repetitions as the heathen do. For they think that they will be heard for their many words"* (Matthew 6:7). This statement implies that communication doesn't equal communion. Many words don't deepen a conversation; they only lengthen it. Lengthy prayers are wonderful, so long as there's depth. Some prayers are a mile wide and an inch deep. God would rather hear prayers that are an inch wide and a mile deep. That's hard for us to fathom because our brains are wired to measure things numerically.

We think short prayers are powerless.

The truth is, only powerless prayers are powerless.

Although God knows how many times you have prayed, I doubt He's keeping score. But *we* can't seem to stop keeping score, tallying up and calculating our lives. When our prayers feel like they don't measure up, "we" feel like we don't measure up, which is why our prayer life must be gospel-driven. The gospel reminds us that it's not our spiritual score or performance that qualifies us to know God, but Jesus Christ who died on the cross, was buried and resurrected.

I'm not urging you to shorten or lengthen your prayers, but to deepen them. Whether you pray 15 minutes, 30 minutes or an hour a day is not what concerns me. The heart of the matter is how you pray, and if your prayers flow from guilt or grace—human effort or the Holy Spirit.

Hebrews 4:16 says, *"Let us therefore come boldly to the throne of grace, that we may find mercy and grace in the time of need."* This is more than a permission slip, but a VIP pass into God's throne room. Think of all the attributes that could finish the phrase "the throne of…" The writer of this verse could have easily described God's throne as "the throne of truth" or "the throne of power" (which are both true). Instead, it's "the throne of grace," telling us that when we come to God in prayer, He's seated in grace.

No matter where or when we talk to God, He's always in a gracious mood. Grace is the cushion He sits on.

Talking to God is easier when you know He's generally not in a bad mood, nor is He irritated by our daily lives. God wants to talk with you. Every time you connect with God in prayer, you're demonstrating the power of the gospel in the most intimate way. If you've neglected to pray for several days or have even gone silent for weeks, you don't have to cram or pray "make up" prayers to appease God.

The Lord doesn't count your prayers; rather He wants your prayers to count.

Nothing I've said about prayer thus far should suggest that you could treat your prayer life casually or frivolously. I'm not promoting laziness or inconsistency, but simply laying the foundation for how we connect with God in real life. We always rush to the *practice* of prayer without realizing the *premise* of prayer. Remember, it's all about relationship. We shouldn't pray *so* that God will love us, but *because* He loves us.

When Paul encourages us to *"pray without ceasing"* (1 Thess. 5:17), He's not calling us to drop everything and pray all day long. Rather, this is a call to develop a prayer life, a continuous conversation with God. It's through that avenue of daily conversation where God can guide us away from temptation and closer to His purpose.

Lead Me Not into Temptation

In the Lord's Prayer, Jesus taught us to pray *"do not lead us into temptation, but deliver us from the evil one"* (Matt. 6:13). This is an interesting prayer because it seems to imply that God *can* lead us into temptation. Why would we need to pray for something to happen ("lead us not"), unless the opposite was true?

Does God lead us into temptation?

That notion would appear to disagree with James 1:13, which says, *"When tempted, no one should say, "God is tempting me." For God cannot be tempted by evil, nor does he tempt anyone."*

On the other hand, the Bible reveals, *"Then Jesus was led by the Spirit into the wilderness to be tempted by the devil"*

(Matt. 4:1). This scripture suggests that the Holy Spirit leads us into temptation.

So the question is, does He or does He not lead us into temptation? Allow me to explain the answer. God doesn't tempt us, but He can lead us *towards* or *away* from temptation. God doesn't do the tempting, satan does. Here's the logic: God is the trainer that brings us into the arena to fight, but He's not the opponent we face.

We don't always know why God leads us into tempting situations, but we know it builds our endurance and reveals His faithfulness in our lives.

The Bible teaches, *"No temptation has overtaken you except what is common to mankind. And God is faithful; he will not let you be tempted beyond what you can bear. But when you are tempted, he will also provide a way out so that you can endure it"* (1 Cor. 10:13).

Although the Holy Spirit may lead you into tempting situations, it's only to strengthen your faith, to refine your character by giving you a choice between right and wrong.

Your prayer life is the most powerful way to navigate through the thick jungle of temptation. The more consistent your prayers are, the more you'll hear from God. And the more you hear from God, the more He'll guide you. Jesus said, *"Watch and pray so that you will not fall into temptation…"* (Matt. 26:41).

Prayer is not going to "temptation-proof" your life, but it will enhance your vision. Through prayer, you will see a clearer picture of the enemy's land mines. It is absolutely essential that you develop and maintain a prayerful relationship with Jesus. Quite simply, we need to pray because we need the presence of God. It's the lifeline of our faith.

Spiritual vs. Spirit-Led

One of the reasons why prayer is difficult is because many have a flawed view of spirituality. We have the tendency to segment our lives into these little compartments …family, spiritual, work, social, recreation. We try to neatly segregate these areas by promoting the concept of: God first, family second, then work, school, and so on.

Sounds good on the surface.

However, this concept prevents us from seeing that all of our lives are fully integrated and intertwined. To suffer in one area of life…affects all areas of life. That's why we call in sick to work when our physical bodies aren't feeling well. My physical health will affect my ability to focus at work. It's all connected – mind, body and soul.

Our compartments are simply an artificial way of trying to balance things out. But the truth is, all these compartments cross over and collide – which is why Jesus must be at the core of our entire lives.

In the Hebrew language, there is no word for "spiritual." Jesus also never used the term "spiritual life" or "spirituality." So it's probably not a good idea for us to view our spiritual activity as our "spiritual life." This dangerously allows us to "be spiritual" when it's time to pray, worship or serve, but be "not so spiritual" when it's time to work or play. The reality is that God wants to saturate every corner of our lives with His presence.

If you view your relationship with God as your "spiritual life," then it's easier to shelve prayer on a spiritual bookshelf – pick up and drop off when needed. Scheduling a time to pray is perfectly fine if it's part of an ongoing conversation you're having with God.

I'm more concerned that people talk to God in "prayer" and disconnect the rest of the day. I believe we need to view all aspects of life as having a spiritual element, or a place for God to dwell, not so we can over-spiritualize the common, but to maintain an awareness of God's presence.

Part of our problem is that we get extra-spiritual for church on Sunday, while being spiritually neutral the rest of the week. We've programmed ourselves to turn our spirituality on and off.

Jesus prayed, *"Your kingdom come, your will be done, on earth as it is in heaven"* (Matthew 6:10). Heaven is supposed to invade our lives, permeate everything we do – even the "non-spiritual" stuff. It's that atmosphere that has the greatest potential to impact the world around us.

I've discovered that prayer is more than a moment; it's a continuous conversation with God that happens throughout my day. The more I talk to God during the day, the more aware I am of His presence. And the more aware I am of His presence, the more confident I am in the face of temptation and trouble.

The apostle Paul taught: *"Walk by the Spirit, and you will not gratify the desires of the flesh"* (Galatians 5:16). Walking denotes a journey or a pace. It's a metaphor for life. Living by the Spirit is different then trying to act or be spiritual (by doing spiritual things). The former is about having a Spiritual frame of mind – one that is connected to God.

Walking by the Spirit is about living out of the Divine nature that God has given us through the infilling of the Holy Spirit.

Of course, this doesn't mean that your flesh is powerless and the fight is over. As long as your heart beats, you will have to deal with the flesh. Paul continued to write, *"For the flesh desires what is contrary to the Spirit, and the Spirit what is contrary to the flesh. They are in conflict with each other, so that you are not to do whatever you want"* (verse 17). As hopeless as this scenario seems, there is way to gain an advantage over temptation and our fleshly cravings. Don't settle for a stalemate between The Spirit and the flesh, or call it a tie game. Paul concluded *"But if you are led by the Spirit, you are not under the law"* (verse 18).

There is not a need for spiritual believers, but for *Spirit-led* believers.

This may sound odd, but we need less spirituality and more Spirit-ledness. I realize I just made up a word. But it works for me.

Being Spirit-led is allowing the Holy Spirit to influence your daily life. It doesn't mean you have to pray about what color to paint your room or if you should buy Nikes or Reeboks. It means that you live with an awareness of

God's presence and are sensitive to His voice – whether at church, in the office or on the golf course.

Your spirit needs to be awakened to a life where prayer isn't merely a practice or an art form, but a way of living. A Spirit-led mind allows me to talk with my heavenly Father at any moment, for any duration of time – whether in my room, my car or throughout my workday.

In summary, I hope to have given you a fresh perspective on prayer and the role that it plays in our lives. I suppose it would take an entire book to truly dissect this subject. Drawing closer to God in prayer will prepare you to overcome temptation and the cravings of the flesh.

But let's face the truth. Even when we try our best and pray as often as we can, we still stumble and fall short of God's glory. We still mess up. We all take the bait from time to time. So then, how do we bounce back after a fall? How do we deal with our sin in a biblical and God-honoring way? Read the next chapter to find out.

8

Breaking your Silence

Finding Freedom through Confession

I've devoted seven chapters of this book on how to overcome and resist temptation. But let's be real. We all fail and give in to temptation—even if it's just eating chocolate cake when you're on a diet. Of course, some sins carry bigger consequences than others, but we must recognize our flawed humanity. We also must realize that our shortcomings never surprise God. He knows you better than you know yourself.

We all fall short.

Maybe you have fallen recently and feel like God can't forgive you, or that your life is worthless now. Maybe you're holding on to guilt for something you did in your past, something you can't seem to shake loose. Maybe you've failed your spouse, your children or your coworkers.

If you feel encaged by a past failure or recent sin in your life, you need to know that God is faithful and just to forgive. The key is that you must be sincere and ready to change.

But...maybe that's problem.

Maybe you're sorry for what you did (or doing), but not ready to make things right, or you're looking for an easy escape hatch, a quick-fix scripture to bail you out and help you feel better about yourself.

Most times people want relief from feeling guilty, but not restitution for their wrongdoings.

In other words, they want to *feel* better, not *be* better. But as I hope to show you in this chapter, there's a big difference between feeling better and being better, between feeling sorry and repenting.

Sinsurance

Confession is a good thing. Actually, it's a great thing – if done in the proper way. True confession in Christ holds the promise of forgiveness, freeing the heart from guilt and breaking the shackles of shame. One of the most well-known Bible verses is 1 John 1:9: *"If we confess our sins, he is faithful and just and will forgive us our sins and purify us from all unrighteousness."* I love this verse. Who wouldn't? It offers what I call "sinsurance" – insurance that covers our sins when we seek God's forgiveness.

Through genuine confession, we immediately experience four of God's promises. Let's a take quick look at each one.

Promise #1 – Faithfulness

The Bible teaches that God is "faithful" to forgive. In this text, the Greek word for "faithful" is *pistos,* which implies that God is trustworthy and reliable. You can depend on God to forgive. Sometimes we view God through the same lenses we view others or ourselves and so we assume that He's not always ready to forgive. As humans, we don't naturally want to forgive when we're offended or hurt by someone. We say things like: "I'm in the *process* of forgiving that person." "I'm on the road to forgiveness." "I'm not ready to forgive." Although we ought to forgive quickly, our emotions can get in the way.

God is different than us in this regard.

His forgiveness is never a process. He doesn't hold back His mercy and grace. God never has to *get ready to forgive*, because Jesus already went to the cross to set us free from sin and condemnation. He is faithful and unwavering, no matter how dirty your life feels or how many times you've fallen down. God doesn't get tired of forgiving, either. He's not looking down at you saying, "You're wearing me out with your little problems."

The more aware you are of God's faithfulness, the more confident you'll be about life. Now of course, there is a danger in taking God's faithfulness and grace for granted. Although God is faithful to forgive, we shouldn't abuse His grace with utter disregard and avid sinning simply because we know He'll forgive us (ref. Romans 5:20-6:2). God is faithful, but He's not interested in playing games. While His grace and faithfulness doesn't run out, time does. Don't be a buzzer beater Christian, banking your salvation on a last second prayer of repentance. Habitual sin and its consequences may eject you out of the game.

Promise #2 – Justice

1 John 1:9 also tells us that God is *"just and will forgive our sins."* The Greek word for "just" is *dikaios*, which means judicial approval. This implies that God is judicially righteous in His judgments and decisions. When God forgives or blesses, it's lawful because He's the final authority and cannot contradict Himself. God is just, and through the death, burial and resurrection of Jesus Christ, we're justified as His sons and daughters. As blood-washed believers, we are made just in the eyes of God (even though we may sin and fall short).

According to Romans 4:35, *"He was delivered over to death for our sins and was raised to life for our justification."* God is just. He's lawfully correct to forgive us because of the finished work of Jesus on the cross. When we seek His forgiveness and mercy, we are already in a lawful position to ask. You shouldn't hang your head low and live in oppression because of a sin you committed.

The enemy will certainly accuse and condemn you. He will rub your past in your face. He will attack your self-worth and remind you of how bad or messed up you are. But grab a hold of this truth. God is just! He is legally cleared to forgive you and there's nothing the devil or any demon in hell can do about it. You are justified. Or as it's been said, justification by Jesus means it is "just-if-I'd" never sinned.

Promise #3 – Forgiveness

We read in Ephesians 1:7, *"In him we have redemption through his blood, the forgiveness of sins, in accordance with the riches of God's grace."* As born-again believers, God simply sees the atoning blood of Jesus Christ on our lives and therefore He is faithful, just and prompt in His forgiveness.

Until Jesus returns for His Church and as long as you're alive on this earth, anytime you seek His forgiveness – you got it. That's grace in action. When God forgives you, He doesn't keep record. Look at these startling words from Hebrews 8:12, *"For I will forgive their wickedness and will remember their sins no more."* You might want to read that verse again. Maybe a third time so it really sinks in.

Does God really forgive *and* forget?

Is that even possible?

If we take Hebrews 8:12 literally, then we must come to that conclusion. I don't doubt God's all-knowingness. There isn't anything past, present or future that He doesn't know. What this verse conveys is God's unwillingness to remember, or His ability to block out what He wishes to block out. That ability is nearly impossible for us as humans. We try hard to forget, to block out memories, but it never works. However, God forgets what He wants to forget. Here are more scriptures to reinforce this truth.

- "You will again have compassion on us; you will tread our sins underfoot and hurl all our iniquities into the depths of the sea" (Micah 7:19).
- "I, even I, am he who blots out your transgressions, for my own sake, and remembers your sins no more" (Isaiah 43:25).

When God forgives you, He doesn't change His mind later. He doesn't come to you and say "Oh, never mind, you messed up too badly last time, so I'm going to remember that again." When you know this truth, it will affect how you move forward after falling into temptation.

If you believe that God is holding you captive, then you won't live in the freedom of the gospel.

God doesn't need to take a poll in heaven or consider opposing arguments. His forgiveness is automatic to those who confess and repent. Don't let anyone convince you otherwise. If God forgives you, then you can stand on that promise.

However, God's forgiveness doesn't solve the grief He feels when we sin. His forgiveness doesn't negate His displeasure over your sin.

Promise #4 – Purification

Last but not least, 1 John 1:9 reveals that if we confess our sins, God will *"purify us from all unrighteousness."* Maybe this promise is the grand finale, the crescendo of confession. Not only does God forgive your sins, but He scrubs out the residue of unrighteousness that separates us from Him.

To be righteous is to be *in right standing* before God, and expresses the idea of a healthy relationship.

Confession allows the Holy Spirit to sanctify your life for a closer relationship with God. Many Christians skip this step. We usually seek forgiveness to relieve our conscience (feel better about ourselves), not realizing that God is calling us to purity – a life of practical inward and outward holiness. God commands us to live holy, separated unto Him (ref. 1 Peter 1:16).

The ultimate goal of confession and repentance is to repair our relationship with God and become more like Him. If we dodge the purifying process, we're stopping short and limiting what God can do in us.

Purifying is also a process that involves our participation.

As God initiates purification in our lives, we, through the power of the Holy Spirit, are to continue the process and take out our own trash. The Bible teaches, *"All who have this hope in him purify themselves, just as he is pure"* (1 John 3:3).

We need to take action and responsibility for our personal purity.

Like washing your hands, you don't have the power to create cleanness, but you're empowered to apply it— through the lifestyle convictions and spiritual boundaries you draw.

Admission vs. Confession

Usually, our confession is more like a simple admission of guilt, without taking responsibility for our actions: "Yes, Dad, I broke your watch." "Yes, dear, I ate your slice of pie." "Yes, sir, I was late to work." That kind of admission feels relieving for a moment, but doesn't address the deeper issues we hide. At the beginning of this book, I shed light on Samson's "secret struggles" (secret lions) that he hid from his family. This was a dangerous pattern that ultimately forced him to lead a double-life. You can't afford to play that game.

Admission doesn't require a full confession, and therefore doesn't have the same affect. If my wife questioned me about eating a slice of pie, I could admit by simply nodding my head "yes," showing her the crumbs on my shirt, or simply saying "Yes dear, I did." It's a start, but not the entire story. A full confession would be to tell her when I took the slice, how often I've been doing it and a sincere apology – for taking the slice or lying about it.

While admission acknowledges wrongdoing, confession takes responsibility for it.

I'm concerned that too many Christians are confusing the two and feel content with just admitting their sins. The whole "I'm human and make mistakes" is a true sentiment, but shouldn't cancel our responsibility to make things right.

Our sins are washed, but our consequences aren't.

For example, Jesus can forgive the sin of murder. But the consequence of murder is usually a prison sentence. That's a consequence for taking someone's life. Jesus will forgive your greed but He's not going to simply cancel your credit card debt. You need to make those payments and work out a financial plan. Jesus paid the debt of our sins, not our credit cards.

Jesus can forgive the sin of fornication. But the consequences can be pregnancy and raising a child. That is not something you can avoid and leave "under the blood." The blood of Jesus won't raise your children for you. You have to take responsibility for that action and make huge adjustments.

Jesus will forgive you if you've offended or hurt someone. But whether they forgive you is another story. It may take time to rebuild trust and earn your place back into someone's life.

Forgiveness is prompt, but restitution is a process. Forgiveness does not erase our need to take responsibility for what we have done. Therefore, confession initiates the process of forgiveness, healing and restitution. We must come clean, not just in the privacy of our minds, but to those we've hurt and to our brothers and sisters in Christ.

The English definition of *confession* is to admit to, or acknowledge something. But as I've explained, God's definition goes further. He sees confession as a process that leads to lifestyle changes.

The Dangers of Unconfessed Sins

King David was transparent about the problems he experienced regarding unconfessed sin. He, of course, was no stranger to falling into temptation and sinning, as I described in an earlier chapter. But what he wrote in Psalm 32 reveals the dangerous affects of secret sins. Verses 3-5 (NLT) say, *"When I refused to confess my sin, my body wasted away, and I groaned all day long. Day and night your hand of discipline was heavy on me. My strength evaporated like water in the summer heat. Finally, I confessed all my sins to you and stopped trying to hide my guilt. I said to myself, "I will confess my rebellion to the Lord." And you forgave me! All my guilt is gone."*

According to David's psalm, unconfessed sin produces three types of sickness. Let's take a look at each one.

1. Physical Sickness

David said (verse 3), *"When I refused to confess my sin, my body wasted away, and I groaned all day long."* David was under such intense stress that it seems he could barely get out of bed. His body throbbed with pain. There is no question that unconfessed sins take a toll on the physical body. The stress of living with a secret will eat away at your mind and affect your health in untold ways.

Our bodies weren't designed to carry the weight of sin. We were designed to live in the perfection of God's presence, in a sinless world. Thanks Adam and Eve, that's all changed. But that's why Jesus went to the Cross – to take away our sins and give us eternal life.

David found physical relief through full confession. I'm not a doctor and can't give you medical advice. But there's a possibility that your health's decline is related to your unconfessed sin – if you, in fact, are living with that issue. David said he "groaned all day long." He couldn't escape his conscience. Don't allow sin to deteriorate your mental and physical health.

God won't heal what we won't reveal. The Bible says, *"Therefore confess your sins to each other and pray for each other so that you may be healed"* (James 5:6). This is true for both physical and emotional healing. Experiencing God's healing power starts with total honesty about your condition or situation. The truth won't bless a lie. So, if you're hiding a sin or addiction, step out and experience real victory in Jesus Name.

2. Spiritual Sickness

David said (verse 4), *"Day and night your hand of discipline was heavy on me. My strength evaporated like water in the summer heat."* These are the words of a man who is spiritually sick, incapable of enjoying the benefits of God's presence. David was living with heaviness in his spirit, because he knew that God wasn't pleased with him.

When you don't confess your sins and repent, you become spiritually dehydrated. Your strength evaporates. The spiritually sick person becomes disillusioned and works extra hard to make his or her Christian life work –

to no avail. No matter how hard you try to serve God with unconfessed sin, you will quickly burnout, become angry or simply give up. You could also become disgruntled with the Church or its leadership and feel abused when corrected or asked to obey spiritual authority. Some general symptoms of spiritual sickness could include:

- **Focus on self** – When your spiritual health breaks down, you don't care about anything else but you – your hurts, desires, and goals. You stop caring about God and other people. You want the attention, the pity of others, but are not willing to help someone else.

- **Loss of appetite** – Jesus said, *"Blessed are those who hunger and thirst for righteousness, for they will be filled"* (Matthew 5:6). A sign of sickness is the loss of hunger or thirst. Whenever I get sick, I can't eat right. Nothing tastes good. Everything is bland. In the Spirit, hunger and passion is essential to receiving God's blessings and promises. So if you've lost your hunger for God's Word or His presence, maybe your unconfessed sin has made you spiritually sick.

- **Loss of functions** – When you're sick, your body stops functioning effectively. Sometimes I get so sick with the flu that I can't even get out of bed. And if I do, I can barely walk because I feel so dizzy. In the Spirit, you also stop functioning properly as a member of the body of Christ. You stop doing what God has called you to do, or simply become ineffective at it.

If you notice any of these symptoms popping up in your life, maybe you're concealing a sin or unhealthy habit. Perhaps you're thinking, "Wait a minute, wouldn't I know if I were living with a sin? Wouldn't it be obvious?" The answer is…*not always.*

I'm reminded of David's prayer: *"Search me, O God, and know my heart; Try me, and know my anxieties; And see if there is any wicked way in me, And lead me in the way everlasting"* (Psalm 139:23-24, NKJV). This prayer implies that sometimes we're not fully aware of what lurks in our hearts. Time passes and we assume that all is well. But that's when we must ask God to search us deeply and reveal anything that is unholy or unconfessed.

If God were to run a spiritual x-ray on your heart, what would He find? Is your soul at risk? Is your faith on life-support?

Spiritual sickness leads to spiritual deadness.

You can go to church, give offerings and sing in the choir, and still be spiritually dead. Stop living like a zombie! In that condition, you will never experience an abundant life. It's time to wake up, repent and strengthen what remains of your faith (read Revelation 3:1-3). The Holy Spirit will empower you to stomp out the sickness in your soul. It's time to thrive and live as a blood-washed believer – forgiven and accepted by your Savior Jesus Christ.

3. Emotional Sickness

David continued to write (verse 5): *"Finally, I confessed all my sins to you and stopped trying to hide my guilt. I said to myself, 'I will confess my rebellion to the Lord.' And you forgave me! All my guilt is gone."* For the entire duration of his unconfessed sin, guilt wrapped its tail around David and squeezed the life out of him. He tried to mask his guilt and pretend everything was fine, but realized that he really had nowhere to hide – just like Adam after he ate the fruit.

Many believers are caught in the grip of guilt and struggle with it on a daily basis. Unfortunately, some even believe that guilt is virtuous and leads to a healthy Christian life. This fallacy stems from the notion that the more demeaned we are, the holier we are – which is a total misunderstanding of godly conviction.

Allow me to clarify this issue. Conviction comes as the Holy Spirit exposes the gap between our behavior and God's standard. True conviction should lead to true confession. When conviction stirs our hearts, there is a need to confess, repent and find God's forgiveness. At that exact moment, the issue is settled and forgiven.

Guilt is different. It's a crippling emotion that keeps you from moving forward. Guilt does not produce the freedom that comes through conviction and confession. Instead, it chokes us and leaves us feeling condemned – frozen by past mistakes. While feeling guilty, you are incapable of being fully present, fully attune to God's voice and will for your life. Guilt sucks the joy out of life, feeds your worst fears and could strain your most important relationships.

Are you wrestling with guilt over an unconfessed sin or unsettled issue in your life? Are you ashamed to admit a secret struggle of yours? Do you fear the consequences of coming clean about your personal battles and shortcomings? Like Adam in the garden, our natural tendency is to hide from God.

Instead of hiding *from* God, we must hide *in* God.

Romans 8:1 says, *"Therefore, there is now no condemnation for those who are in Christ Jesus."* Guilt was crushed at the cross. Its grip was broken. But to experience that freedom from guilt, to apply the power of the Gospel to your life, you must be ready to confess and repent.

If the Holy Spirit has been convicting you, you must take action and exercise the freedom you have in Jesus Christ. Don't allow that lying lion – satan – to deceive you another day. In the next chapter, I'm going to share some powerful truths about killing the lions that intimidate you – the ones you've been afraid to face. If you're ready, keep reading.

LYING LIONS

10

Lion Killers

Facing your Fears with Courage

Defeating temptation can be a scary process depending on your situation. Over the course of my life, I've noticed that temptation and fear often go hand-in-hand. My fears are usually accompanied by the temptation to quit, to complain or to self-indulge in something that isn't healthy.

On the flip end, my temptations attract certain fears, like the fear of failing or repeating the same mistake. Fears come in all shapes and sizes. But they all have the potential to destroy our lives.

The Bible says in 1 Peter 5:8, *"Be alert and of sober mind. Your enemy the devil prowls around like a roaring lion looking for someone to devour."* This imagery of the devil as a roaring lion should alert us all to the evil that lurks.. We all have to contend with lions—issues that rule by intimidation. Unlike the lion with the honey that Samson touched, your lion may still be fully alive—roaring and prowling around.

You must know your fears and how to conquer them.

Everybody wants to be conquerors.

Few want to be confronters.

You cannot conquer what you will not confront. If you're going to overcome your fears, you must face them down.

I'm reminded of Proverbs 26:13, which says, *"The lazy man says, "There is a lion in the road! A fierce lion is in the streets!"'* The man in this Proverb was living in fear. A lion was prowling around his house and rather than become its next meal, he chose to stay inside.

Seems logical, right? Well, maybe not.

This Proverb is an analogy that reveals how timid people deal with their fears. Rather then facing their fears with bold decisions or courageous faith, they hide behind the curtains of excuses and try to block out their fears. Blocking out your fears is not the same as confronting them. You can try to mentally block out the things you're afraid of and tiptoe through life. Or you can rely on the power of God's Spirit to face what frightens you.

The man in the Proverb allowed external lions to control his internal peace. Judging by the volume of his plea – the verse records two exclamation points – he's in no better condition then if he was on the street. Even behind closed doors, he's still afraid. His efforts to avoid the lions failed miserably because the lions were not just in the streets, but also in his own head. Once the lions got in his head (his thoughts), it didn't matter where they roamed. His home environment wasn't any calmer by playing it safe.

He ate…while thinking about lions.

He slept or stayed up…while thinking about lions.

He tried to live normally…while still thinking about lions.

See the problem here? Avoiding the lions that lurked only worsened his fears. So often, we attempt to block out our fears, but find very little solace. If the enemy can create the illusion that your lions are too powerful, he can get the same reaction as an actual threat. The devil doesn't have to attack you if he can convince you that you're already defeated. But it's time to separate fact from fiction. You are more than a conqueror through Christ who loves you (ref. Romans 8:37).

The man in the Proverb also suffered from what I call the "Someday Syndrome"—a condition of procrastination and laziness. He was called a *lazy man* because obviously, he was not only paralyzed by fear, but by his own apathy. His conscious was partly soothed by the fantasy that "someday" he would face those fierce lions and teach them a lesson. This is how we cope with our fears without actually facing them—by promising ourselves that we will do something about it, someday.

Dear reader...that "someday" is here right now.

Jesus didn't die for us to play it safe. He died to make us hell's worst nightmare.

We cannot be like the man in the proverb and just settle into our comfort zones and hold down the fort. We can't peek through the windows of mediocrity and expect God to move.

When we move, He'll move.

Rather than live another day with the false hope of things getting better, step out of your excuses and confront the lions that keep lying to you! Here's the best part, you don't have to try this on your own. The Holy Spirit will empower you and be your guide. Remember what 2 Timothy 1:7 says: *"For God has not given us a spirit of fear, but of power and of love and of a sound mind."*

The Courage of a Lion Killer

I would like to introduce you to an Old Testament hero named Benaiah, a man who exhibited great courage by killing a lion on a snowy day. His act of bravery is recorded in 2 Samuel 23:20: *"Benaiah son of Jehoiada, a valiant fighter from Kabzeel, performed great exploits. He struck down Moab's two mightiest warriors. He also went down into a pit on a snowy day and killed a lion."* Benaiah was a man's man – a toughly built warrior who didn't back down in the face of adversity.

Unlike Samson who had supernatural bursts of power, Benaiah was expertly trained and had developed a skillset that turned him into a human weapon.

Had I been in Benaiah's shoes on that day, I'm not sure I would have been as brave. Okay, let's be honest. There's no way I would have chased a lion into a pit! But hypothetically speaking, if I had actually conjured up the courage to hunt a real lion, I certainly would not have picked a snowy day – where it's impossible to run. After a few steps, my narrow feet would sink knee-deep into the snow.

Maybe that's what faith and courage are all about. Maybe God is asking you to step out far enough that you can't retreat so easily. Perhaps you've been avoiding a challenge because it requires that you let go of your escape hatches.

Maybe God is trying to remove your "Plan B" to show you that His "Plan A" is much better.

This you can bet on: conditions will never be perfect before you step into your purpose. It's time to let go of that false expectation. God is looking for someone who will have the tenacity of Benaiah, who will fight the good fight of faith, who will stand up when others sit down, who will speak up when others stay silent, who will trust and follow Jesus with reckless abandon.

Don't listen to your nerves, which signal that you're too afraid. Listen to the Voice of the Spirit that calls you into the deep.

You might be afraid, but you won't be alone.

Personally, I don't think I've ever felt "ready" to do the things that God has called me to do – whether it was to preach my first message at the age of 17, write my first book at the age of 22, or lead my family as a strong husband and father. I certainly didn't feel 100% ready when God called me to launch CityLight Church in Mountain View, California. I knew where God was calling me, but that didn't settle all my nerves. It hit me that I was about to embark on a journey that would forever change my life.

Since I grew up in a pastor's home, I saw firsthand the challenges and struggles that pastors have to endure. I also saw my hero, my dad, exemplify extraordinary courage and wisdom during his pastorship. Maybe that's why I was afraid. I didn't think I had "it". At one point, it felt like my life was missing a special "pastor's gene" and that I wouldn't be able to measure up.

But I was wrong.

It wasn't until after I heeded the call of God on my life that I began to realize that faith isn't the absence of fear, but the courage to respond in spite of it.

Presently, CityLight Church is now a year old. God has allowed us to reach a diverse group of people in our city and communities. We're still at the beginning stages, but I share this to encourage you, to remind you that courage isn't blocking out your fears—it's facing them.

The Making of a Lion Killer

The fact that Benaiah didn't experience the same type of superhuman strength and invincibleness of Samson meant that he was also more vulnerable in battle. However, Benaiah lived a life that prepared him for greatness, one that would eventually promote him as one of King David's mighty men – an ancient prototype of the modern-day Secret Service. Benaiah did more than sparring in the gym and perfecting his moves. He went through spiritual formation and training.

The Bible doesn't narrate Benaiah's whole life, but it gives us just enough to catch a glimpse of who he was. I would like to share some life principles based on Benaiah. If you ever want to kill the lions of fear and temptation in your life, the following are truths you must live by and incorporate into your thinking.

1. What you Exalt, you Expand

Benaiah prepared himself to kill lions, not only through physical training, but also through spiritual training. The scriptures mention a small, but significant detail about Benaiah that gave him the upper hand in all his battles—whether against beasts or men. Benaiah was a worshipper.

1 Chronicles 16:6 says, *"Benaiah and Jahaziel the priests regularly blew the trumpets before the ark of the covenant of God."*

Not only could Benaiah fight like a pro, he could play that trumpet like a pro! He had the privilege of blowing the trumpet before the Ark of the Covenant – the presence of God. This is just my opinion; but I believe that Benaiah's time spent as a worshipper prepared him for the challenges he faced in life.

Something special happened whenever Benaiah played his instrument: his focus on God would magnify. Worship brings you into closer proximity to God.

Unfortunately, the opposite is also true. If you worship your problems by complaining or worrying all the time, you enlarge their influence in your life. If you worship your wounds by always feeling sorry for yourself or dwelling on the past, they will appear larger in your life. Just like worship magnifies God, worrying magnifies your problems.

Benaiah chased a lion because he didn't see a large ferocious lion; he saw a house cat. His worshipping lifestyle gave him a God's eye view of what we normally consider to be impossible.

I wonder what would change in your life if you began to elevate your worship and press further into God's presence? I wonder how you would view your problems and your fears if you declared praises instead of complaints? I don't mean to sound insensitive, but could it be that some of your worries are blown out of proportion? I suggest that worshipping God not only enlarges His influence, but it shrinks your enemy's influence.

2. What Forms you, Transforms you

In addition to being a great worshipper, Benaiah lived with the revelation of who he was. This was not a man who suffered from low self-esteem or insecurity. Don't get me wrong. He wasn't perfect. We don't know all the mistakes he made in his life. But when it came to killing lions, he was definitely sure about his God-given identity. In fact, the very mention of his name would remind him of how significant he was. The name Benaiah means "formed by God." That alone suggests that he rarely, if ever, questioned his originality.

Truth be told, many people wrestle with deep insecurity. Maybe you're one of those who struggle to accept yourself and agonize over your imperfections. Maybe you project confidence outwardly, but secretly battle with feelings of inadequacy – at work, at church or even at home.

You should know that God didn't make a mistake when he formed you. Even your imperfections shape the person that God created you to be. You're not an accident. Your heavenly Father formed you inside your mother's womb and anticipated your arrival on this earth. He was the unseen witness in the hospital room who celebrated your birth and smiled at your existence.

It's time to live with the real confidence and awareness that you are God's child, uniquely formed to survive in your environment—no matter how bad it seems. Until you accept who you are in Jesus Christ, the lions of life will continue to torment you. Negative experiences or negative people should not define who you are.

Face your fears with the revelation of who God is, and who He's made you to be. Your life could be radically transformed just by realizing who formed you. The God, who formed you, can transform you into a lion killer.

3. What Scares you, is Scared OF you

Under normal circumstances, lions hunt men. That's why zoos keep lions in cages. But in Benaiah's case, the hunted became the hunter. The Bible says, *"He also went down into a pit on a snowy day and killed a lion."* I'm intrigued by the fact that Benaiah wasn't running from the lion or acted out of self-defense. Honestly, if that were the story, I would still be impressed. Killing a lion out of self-defense is quite a story to tell your grandchildren.

Except, Benaiah ran *towards* the lion, not *away* from it.

Normal people don't chase lions.

Benaiah willfully went on a mission to catch himself a lion. Now, maybe this lion had already caused some havoc in town and had a bounty on its head. Maybe the lion had already struck and took a victim or two. My point is that Benaiah wasn't hunting for lion meat (not sure how that would taste). He was hunting for justice, protection, and peace in his life. He chased the lion because he was driven by a cause. Just like David, who ran towards Goliath and famously declared, "Is there not a cause?"

The lion found itself in an unusual position. It was used to striking fear and overpowering its prey. It was accustomed to roaming freely without any worthy challengers to stand in its way. Today, lions are labeled "king of the jungle" because of how dominant they are. But again, the lion in Benaiah's story was curled up deep inside a cave, hibernating during a snowstorm. Yet it found itself fighting for its life...because one man had enough!

Benaiah didn't wait for the fight to show up on his doorstep. He went looking for a fight.

Maybe that's what we ought to do – instead of sitting around and waiting for the devil to strike, we should take the fight to him. Too often, the church is in protection mode, always reacting to the enemy's moves. I say it's time for believers to get aggressive about their faith and God-given destiny.

No more "Mr. Nice Guy." No more living in the shadows of fear or self-doubt. Psalm 91:13 says, *"You will tread on the lion and the cobra; you will trample the great lion and the serpent."* The lions you face belong under your feet. It's time for you to recognize that what you're scared of…is actually scared of you. Not just because of who you are, but mainly because of Who dwells within you – Jesus Christ. Churches need to wake up. Fathers and mothers need to wake up. Young people need to wake up.

Let's have the attitude of Benaiah and hunt the hunter. Instead of wishing that the devil would play fair, why not terrorize him and the realm of darkness by fulfilling your God-given purpose. The enemy is terrified of you rising up with power and purpose. But that's too bad for him. You are too anointed, too blessed and too beloved by God to sit back and watch your destiny fade in the wind. Take authority over your fears and temptations.

Fear not, because living within you is a greater lion – the Lion of Judah – Jesus Christ! In the final chapter, you'll discover how Jesus has won the victory for you.

11

The Roaring Lamb

Following Jesus into Victory

I am not the hero of this book. Neither are the amazing characters we've learned about. The hero of this book, of our lives, is a Lion who became a Lamb – Jesus Christ. When John the Baptist introduced Jesus, he declared, *"Look, the Lamb of God, who takes away the sin of the world"* (1 John 1:29). Then in Revelation 5:5, we read: *"Then one of the elders said to me, 'Do not weep! See, the Lion of the tribe of Judah, the Root of David, has triumphed. He is able to open the scroll and its seven seals.'"*

The Lamb of God is the Lion of Judah and the Lion of Judah is also the Lamb of God. What does this mean for you and me as followers of Christ? How does it help us overcome temptation and sin?

The Lamb of God

The apostle Paul referred to Jesus as our "Passover Lamb" (ref. 1 Cor. 5:7). This is a reference to the first Passover lamb, whose blood saved the Israelites from death and delivered them from slavery (ref. Exodus 12:12-13). What the Passover lamb did to redeem the Israelites from their bondage to slavery, Jesus – the Lamb of God – did to redeem us from our bondage to sin. The Passover lamb is a foreshadowing of Jesus as the sacrificial lamb.

Lambs are preyed upon; they are harmless, fragile and killed for food. Jesus became our lamb by laying down His life and shedding His precious blood in our place. The Bible teaches, *"For you know that it was not with perishable things such as silver or gold that you were redeemed from the empty way of life handed down to you from your ancestors, but with the precious blood of Christ, a lamb without blemish or defect"* (1 Peter 1:18-19). The lamb reminds us of Jesus' innocence and meekness—that He came not to be served, but to serve.

Like the Passover lamb's blood on the wooden doorposts, Jesus' bloodshed on the wooden cross is the sacrifice for our sins. Jesus fulfilled the Old Testament sacrificial system by becoming the ultimate offering.

When I think of Jesus as the Lamb, I think of His shocking grace and extravagant mercy towards me. As blood-washed believers, we should stand firmly in the gift of God's salvation and not live under the shadow of condemnation. As a child, I remember singing "what can wash away my sins, nothing but the blood of Jesus." Nothing but the saving blood of Jesus can wash a dirty life of sin and render us righteous in God's sight. You can't make it to heaven or make it through this life without being covered by His blood.

The blood is applied when we accept Jesus as our Savior by repenting of our sins and being baptized in Jesus' Name (ref. Acts 2:38).

If you want to find freedom in a world of temptation, you must rely on the Lamb of God. There is a direct link between the blood of the lamb and your daily walk in victory. Revelation 12:11 says, *"They triumphed over him by the blood of the Lamb and by the word of their testimony..."* According to this verse, the key to triumphing over your adversary is being covered by the blood of Jesus and confessing what He's done in your life. You simply must stand in the victory that's already been won for you on the cross.

Perhaps the victory chant of every Christian is found in Revelation 5:12: *"Worthy is the Lamb, who was slain, to receive power and wealth and wisdom and strength and honor and glory and praise!"* Your life is valuable because it cost the Lamb of God His own blood.

Had you been a worthless, lost cause, Jesus never would have been slain for you. Even if you fall and it feels like you're far from God, you can be assured that His love never fails, that His mercy is everlasting, that His grace abounds, that His forgiveness is unlimited – all because the Lamb was slain.

It would take an entire book to explain all the theological truths, types and shadows associated with the lamb. I simply want to declare that your Creator became your Savior by becoming the Lamb of God.

As the Lamb of God, Jesus shed His blood and died on the cross. But that's not the end of the story. As the Lion of

Judah, Jesus rose and conquered hell and death.

As a lamb, He bled. As a lion, He reigns.

The Lion of Judah

For the majority of this book I've used the lion as a symbol of the enemy and his tricks. However, the lions of the enemy are subject to the greater lion. Revelation 5:5 reads: *"Then one of the elders said to me, 'Do not weep! See, the Lion of the tribe of Judah, the Root of David, has triumphed. He is able to open the scroll and its seven seals.'"* Jesus died as a sacrificial lamb, but rose again, and will return as the Lion of Judah.

The origin of this title, "Lion of Judah" is traced to Israel's fourth son whose name was Judah. While Israel was on his deathbed, he gathered all his sons and began to prophesy over their lives. When he got to his son Judah, this is what he said:

"Judah, your brothers will praise you; your hand will be on the neck of your enemies; your father's sons will bow down to you. You are a lion's cub, Judah; you return from the prey, my son. Like a lion he crouches and lies down, like a lioness—who

dares to rouse him? The scepter will not depart from Judah, nor the ruler's staff from between his feet, until he to whom it belongs shall come and the obedience of the nations shall be his. He will tether his donkey to a vine, his colt to the choicest branch; he will wash his garments in wine, his robes in the blood of grapes. His eyes will be darker than wine, his teeth whiter than milk" (Genesis 49:8-12).

The entire passage above wasn't merely a personal word to Judah, but a prophecy about the coming Messiah – Jesus Christ. In this prophecy, there are some key attributes about Jesus, the Lion of Judah. Let's look at a few of them.

1. Praiseworthy

Israel told his son, "Judah, your brothers will praise you." This might have been the most obvious statement. The name Judah actually means "praise." It's no surprise, then, that he would be praised. But this hints to Jesus, who deserves to be praised. In fact, the Bible commands us to praise God. The psalmist said, *"Let everything that has breath praise the Lord"* (Psalm 150:6).

Jesus is the Lion of Judah – the Lion of Praise. Therefore, if we want Him to move in our lives, we must create an atmosphere of praise. King David wrote, *"Yet you are holy, enthroned on the praises of Israel"* (Psalm 22:3). God inhabits the praises of His people. He is attracted to the songs of joy and shouts of praise that we offer Him.

Learn how to praise God no matter what you go through; no matter what season you're in. As you begin to praise and bless His name, you will sense the presence of the Lion of Judah.

Praise is a weapon.

Israel told his son Judah, "Your hand will be on the neck of your enemies." As you praise the Lord, you allow Him to choke the enemies that are trying to destroy you. Remember what I wrote in the previous chapter about Benaiah, a champion who played the trumpet before the ark of God? I can't seem to get that image out of my mind. There is something about praise that moves God and enlarges His influence in our lives.

When we praise God, we are recognizing that it is not our human efforts that produce blessings and prosperity. We come to acknowledge that God holds all things in His hands. Praise has a way of breaking the attitudes of self-sufficiency and pride. It forces us to get our attention on God and off our problems.

Praise takes the focus off the peripheral issues of life. It breaks the mindset of negativity and forces the flesh to rejoice – even when we don't feel like it. Philippians 4:4 tells us to *"rejoice in the Lord always: and again I say, Rejoice."* We don't praise and rejoice because of our problems, we do so *in spite* of our problems.

When we praise, we are actually ministering to the Lord. Although God is complete and self-sustained, He desires that we minister to Him with sounds of praise.

2. Powerful

Israel told his son *"You are a lion's cub, Judah; you return from the prey, my son. Like a lion he crouches and lies down, like a lioness—who dares to rouse him?"* In similar fashion, Jesus (the Lion of Judah) returns from the prey because He is victorious over His opponents. Who or what in its right mind would pick a fight with the Almighty God? He is omnipotent, meaning He is all-powerful. Nothing can stand in His way.

Jeremiah declared: *"Ah, Sovereign Lord, you have made the heavens and the earth by your great power and outstretched arm. Nothing is too hard for you"* (Jeremiah 32:17). Do you believe that nothing is too hard for God? Are you convinced in your heart of God's great power? As the Lamb of God, Jesus made Himself weak and was nailed to a cross. But as the Lion of Judah, Jesus rose from the grave and smashed the power of death.

God doesn't just have power, but all power belongs to Him and flows from His throne. King David said, *"God has spoken once, twice I have heard this: that power belongs to God"* (Psalm 62:11, NKJV). God will never have a power outage. He will never need new batteries or a recharge. His power transcends the cosmos and defies the laws of physics. He sprinkled the universe with stars, ignited the sun's blaze and shaped the world with only His word (ref. Hebrews 11:3).

God's power split the Red Sea in half and allowed the Israelites to walk across dry ground. God's power pulverized the walls of Jericho like a sandcastle and granted victory to His people. His power propelled a little stone to slay a giant named Goliath. His power resurrected a man named Lazarus – whose body was already decomposing.

If you have the Holy Spirit, then that same power lives inside of you.

Jesus told his disciples, *"But you will receive power when the Holy Spirit comes on you; and you will be my witnesses in Jerusalem, and in all Judea and Samaria, and to the ends of the earth"* (Acts 1:8).

Victorious living is more than just avoiding sin and changing your behavior, it's taking your proper place as an empowered, embraced and emboldened child of God. You must walk through this life with the confidence that you are already triumphant. You don't need to ask for victory, you simply must seize it.

3. Pure

Israel told his son Judah that we would *"wash his garments in wine, his robes in the blood of grapes. His eyes will be darker than wine, his teeth whiter than milk."* Again, this verse foreshadows the Messiah. The phrase "robes in the blood of grapes" points to the blood that Jesus would shed on the cross.

Wine is the symbol of His blood. Jesus' body, like grapes, was beaten and crushed until He bled His last drop. But the other phrase that catches my attention is "his teeth whiter than milk."

In the Bible, white is the color that represents purity and holiness. Of the many shades of God's character, nothing compares to the beauty and light of His holiness. God's character is completely perfect and pure. The celestial creatures that surround the throne of God continuously sing, *"Holy, holy, holy is the Lord God Almighty,' who was, and is, and is to come"* (Revelation 4:8).

The creatures don't sing, "loving, loving, loving is the Lord..." They don't sing, "merciful, merciful, merciful is the Lord..." Even though "loving" and "merciful" are both attributes of God, they don't fully express His nature and essence like "holy."

The word "holy" simply means, "set apart or separated." Therefore, when we talk about God's holiness, we're referring to His separateness—the fact that He is perfectly set apart from the evil and sin of this world. God truly is the definition of holy.

The Word of God says, *"But just as he who called you is holy, so be holy in all you do; for it is written: 'Be holy, because I am holy'"* (1 Peter 1:15-16). This small passage contains a big principle. The apostle Peter is reminding us of what God said. We are commanded to be holy, based on the truth that God is holy.

Upon receiving the "Holy" Spirit, we are empowered to live holy as the Spirit leads us through a journey of sanctification – an inward and outward process of separation from the world.

Pursuing holiness is not about being perfect or earning salvation through self-righteousness. It's only through the blood of Jesus (Lamb of God) that we obtain righteousness and holiness. However, we still must take action and do our part to pursue a holy life.

The apostle Paul taught in Romans 12:1-2: *"Therefore, I urge you, brothers and sisters, in view of God's mercy, to offer your bodies as a living sacrifice, holy and pleasing to God—this is your true and proper worship. Do not conform to the pattern of this world, but be transformed by the renewing of your mind. Then you will be able to test and approve what God's will is—his good, pleasing and perfect will."*

Understanding that God is holy and calls us to live holy is essential to living a victorious life. Since holiness is about separation from the world and its system of morality, you must build personal boundaries to ensure that it doesn't mix into your life.

Jesus, the Lion of Judah, is holy, and commands us to pursue a holy life.

Replace your Lying Lion with the Living Lion

I started this book by talking about Samson. So perhaps it's fitting to loop back to this strong man who couldn't resist the honey in the lion's carcass. What Samson didn't realize was that his destiny was sweeter than that honey. What he didn't know, was that one day, another Lion would arise and offer life instead of death. Unlike the lion's carcass in Samson's story, the Lion of Judah (Jesus Christ) didn't stay dead—but rose and is still alive today! Unlike the lion's honey that could only offer temporary satisfaction, the Lion of Judah—the roaring Lamb of God, offers sweetness that never ends.

As the psalmist said: *"How sweet are your words to my taste, sweeter than honey to my mouth!"* (Psalm 119:103). God's promises are sweeter than any honey this world has to offer. Once you get a taste for what Jesus Christ can offer you, nothing else will satisfy – no temptation, no sinful pleasure.

I've realized that my worst day with Jesus is better than my best day without Him. Once you've tasted God's honey, you'll never be able to substitute it for anything else. You'll never be a "happy sinner." Something in you will always crave the honey that flows from God's goodness.

Make a decision that you're going to replace your lying lion with the living Lion.

My purpose for writing this book was to help you find freedom in a world of temptation. My goal was not to write a bunch of do's and don'ts. Rather, to expose the enemy's tactics and reveal God's secrets to living victoriously. Take what you've learned in this book and apply it to your life. Freedom is yours in Jesus Christ – the roaring Lamb.

Acknowledgements

When everything is said and done, I want to live what I write...in my home. My family means everything to me. I want to thank my beautiful wife of twelve years, Cherie, for supporting my ministry and allowing me to write. And thanks to our two children – Makai and Chloe – who inspire and motivate me daily.

I have the privilege of pastoring CityLight Church in Mountain View, CA, and I wouldn't want to be anywhere else. CityLight allows me to fulfill a dual calling – to pastor and to write. A special thanks to our entire staff and core leadership – Ana Pulido, Elizabeth Pulido, and Mario Pulido.

Thanks to my parents, who have always believed in me and made it possible for me to publish my first book – 12 years ago.

Authors write books, but editing and publishing takes a team. Thanks to David Avila, my editor, for treating this book with care and expertise. Finally, thanks to TMG Design Studio, for your creativity and partnership.

About the Author

JACOB M. RODRIGUEZ is the founder and pastor of CityLight Church in Mountain View, California. His dynamic sermons and books reach a virtual audience around the world. He has written seven books, including *The Lord's Lady, Crave,* and *Shift.* Jacob and his wife, Cherie, have two wonderful children, Makai and Chloe.

To learn more about Jacob's ministry, visit his website at www.jacobrodriguez.org. Or to learn more about CityLight Church, visit www.citylightonline.org.

To download a free study guide,
log on to www.lyinglions.com.